Spies Lies and Double

To Phil

Micha...
1/7/2016

To Sue

Enjoy!

Penny e Chris

1

Spies Lies and Double-cross Agents

Spies Lies & Double-cross Agents

Michael A Kushner

Michael working at Bletchley Park
as a volunteer guide

Spies Lies and Double-cross Agents

First published in Great Britain 2017

Published by Michael A Kushner Milton Keynes 2017

ISBN 9 780995 722217

Index

The author lecturing on Cunard Queen Mary 2

Introduction *Spies Lies and Double Cross Agents*

After the unexpected demand for my book 'A journey to Station X' I received feedback "when is the next book coming out?" Though I had no initial intention to write again I felt I owed it to my readers to elaborate on certain areas of the murky underworld of spies. *Communications and intelligence.* Is a brief look at the security of messages throughout the ages with an insight to the foundations of the British Secret Service. *Operation Mincemeat* shows how the British intelligence services during World War II bamboozled the German spy network the *Abwehr*, which led to the enemy believing of an incredible deception. *The Spy Who Loved Himself* was one of the most unlikely characters to work for the British secret service. He was a thief, a liar, a womaniser and a hero but the secret services on both sides never really quite knew who he was actually working for. *The Fifth Man* this is truly an unbelievable story of a Cambridge intellectual who was a communist and worked for Britain's most secret establishment at Bletchley Park during World War II, though he was in fact a spying for Russia. *Spies Lies and Double Cross Agents* is an enhanced look at how British intelligence used Germany's spies. Some who volunteered their services and some who didn't, they then worked for Britain against Germany. A process which in no doubt, would have cost them their lives with one simple slip-up on either side. But they became an integral part of Operation Overlord, D-Day. *The Enigma of the Enigma*, as a guide and lecturer at Bletchley Park, I tell the story of how, when and where the German cipher machine Enigma was broken by the British. [Previously by Polish codebreakers] This chapter is a basic look at the history of the Enigma machine and why the Germans took it on-board in 1926. The Germans considered the Enigma absolutely unbreakable. I have shown here a very basic view of how the German military Enigma machine worked and how it was broken. Hopefully this will remove some of the mystique.

Acknowledgements

Bletchley Park Trust. National Archives. British Library London. Imperial War Museum London. Bundesarchiv Germany.

The Library at Bletchley Park re-created as it was in 1939 Bletchley Park Trust

Communication & Intelligence.

This chapter covers three sections: the history of communications, early code breaking organisations, and the secret intelligence service commonly known as MI6.

When we talk of signals intelligence we are not referring to intelligence in an academic sense. Any interception of signals or the knowledge of your presumed enemy for your own security is known as intelligence in this instance. At its most basic it can be a person putting a glass to their ear against the wall of an adjoining house, listening or spying on the next door neighbour's conversations or hacking into someone's telephone line, or just being a nosy neighbour. If you use that information or pass it on to a third party, this is intelligence for good or for bad.

Since the earliest days of man, when the main way of communicating over any distance was by beating a drum or sending smoke signals, messages could be intercepted. In 500 BCE smoke signals were used to send communications along the Great Wall of China. In 200 BCE the Greek historian Polybius devised a system of visual smoke signals that formed an alphabet, by introducing a cryptographic grid of letters and numbers. The words *Kryptos*, from the Greek, means hidden or secret and *Graphin* is writing. So cryptographic, cryptology, cryptanalyst.

9

Pigeons are known for their ability to home and they have been used for centuries to carry messages for man. During World War II long distance bomber aircrafts would always carry pigeons in case the plane was brought down and unable to send a radio message to their base, when a pigeon with a message attached to its leg would be released and hopefully return to England and pinpoint the location of the unfortunate aircrew. Even our agents (Spies) would use pigeons to send secret messages back to Britain, though these messages were in code. The Germans would try to shoot the pigeons down in an attempt to intercept their messages. During World War II if you were caught with pigeons by the enemy, the punishment would be severe.

Long distance semaphore was used for sending messages by flag or by a machine, using relay stations. This could convey information across very long distances. These messages could be intercepted by prying eyes. So there was a need to send messages in code, which we will cover later.

In 1516 Britain had to protect its delivery of messages and letters from theft and interception. King Henry VIII established the postal system and created the position of Master of the Posts. This was to become Postmaster general in 1710. The idea of a Royal mail system was that messages and letters could be sent and protected by the realm and woe betide anybody who tried to intercept the Royal mail.

Highwayman Dick Turpin

"Stand and deliver"

Sending messages by electricity

From the earliest experiments with electricity it was known that electricity could travel at great speeds. Trials were conducted to send communications long distance. An early idea was to have a cable containing a wire for each letter in the alphabet but this idea seemed impractical. The first working telegraph was built by the English inventor Francis Ronalds in 1816 and used static electricity. At the family home Kelmscott House, Hammersmith, London, he set up a complete subterranean system in a 175 yard long trench as well as an eight mile long overhead telegraph. The lines were connected at both ends to revolving dials marked with the letters of the alphabet and electrical impulses sent along the wire were used to transmit messages. Offering his invention to the Admiralty in July 1816, it was rejected as "wholly unnecessary"

There are many claims to the invention of the telegraph. Paul Schilling, born in 1786 in Russia, was experimenting with electric cables in 1832 in St Petersburg: he was successful in sending a message by electromagnetic telegraph from one room to another in his apartment.

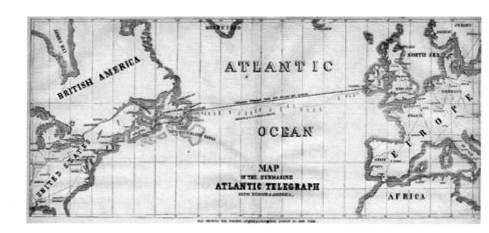

The first successful transatlantic cable was finally laid after a number of attempts in 1865 by the Anglo American Telegraph Company between Heart's Content in Newfoundland and Labrador and Valentia Island near Waterville. In the 1880s, Cyrus Field's Commercial Cable Company laid the first Transatlantic telegraph cable from the nearby townland of Spunkane to Canso, Nova Scotia. The cable station brought much activity to Waterville and increased the town's size

Map of the 1858 Atlantic Cable route from. Frank Leslie's Illustrated

Courtesy Bill Burns www.atlantic –cable.com

In 1837 Samuel Morse independently developed and patented the electric telegraph. A network of cables was laid across the United States and then Britain: communications were achieved by using the new code invented by Samuel Morse and his assistant in 1840. Prior to Morse code the telegraph wire could have had a cable of up to 26 cores, one wire for each letter of the alphabet as in Francis Ronald's system. With Samuel Morse's system you only needed one pair of wires to transmit messages long distance using dots and dashes. Though Samuel Morse was an inventor and painter he will probably only be remembered for his Morse code, at the very beginnings of long distance communications. You could now send messages in real-time, but once you got to the coast, you would still have to use a ship. Experiments were made to make a cable that would be able to withstand being immersed in seawater. In 1849 an electrical engineer working for the South Eastern Railway company laid two miles of specially coated waterproof cable off the coast of Folkestone which was successfully tested with amazing results. It was the Submarine Telegraph Company which laid the first undersea cable link in 1850 between France and England.

With the creation in 1856 of the Anglo American Telegraph Company, the next step was to connect the United States with Britain. A cable was to be laid in 1866 From Valencia Bay West of Ireland to Newfoundland. The problem was the weight of the cable. No ship was large enough to be able to carry the weight. Therefore two ships were used, one from each end and then to meet in the middle of the Atlantic Ocean. The British ship used was Isambard Kingdom Brunel's SS Great Eastern. This was a massive ship that could hold the weight of the enormous cable. Several attempts were initially made but the cable was not strong enough and broke. Eventually she laid 4,200 kilometres (2,600 miles) of transatlantic telegraph cable. A connection was made between the two countries and a transatlantic communications link was at last achieved. Messages that once took months to receive were now received within hours.

Porthcurno in Cornwall became home to the British cable station where submarine cables (cables under the sea) were connected across oceans and throughout the world. Britain had the advantage of routing all its telegraph cables across its Empire, ensuring that no cables or switching stations crossed foreign lands. By the turn of the century most of the world was connected by thousands of miles of submarine cable. Switching and routing stations were dotted all over the globe building an *inter-net*work of communications. The world suddenly became a lot smaller.

In 1872 a telegraph company was created by John Pender, a Scottish submarine cable engineer, through the amalgamation and reorganisation of many existing telegraph companies. The new company became known as the Eastern Telegraph Co (ETC) based at Electra House, Moorgate, London. It was the largest cable operating company in the world. In 1934 it became The Cable & Wireless Company. At its peak it operated 160,000 nautical miles (nm) of cables. John Pender became Chairman of the company on its formation and remained as such until he died in 1896. The General Manager of the company was Sir James Anderson, who had captained the Great Eastern on its Atlantic cable voyages. The company then began to increase its links by duplicating cables over the busiest routes such as the Porthcurno to Carcavelos and Gibraltar. Almost all its cables were manufactured and laid by the Telegraph Construction and Maintenance Company Telcon. (In 1959 the company was acquired by BICC Ltd).

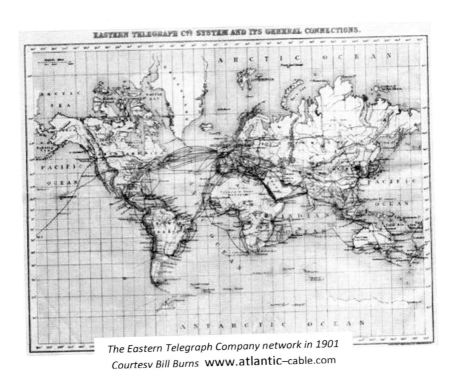

The Eastern Telegraph Company network in 1901
Courtesy Bill Burns www.atlantic–cable.com

Guglielmo Marconi. (25th April 1874–20th July 1937). He was an Italian inventor and electrical engineer known for his pioneering work on long distance radio transmission and for his development of Marconi's law[1] and a radio telegraph system. He is often credited as the inventor of radio, and he shared the 1909 Nobel Prize in Physics with Karl Ferdinand Braun "in recognition of their contributions to the development of wireless telegraphy". Marconi was an entrepreneur, businessman, and founder of The Wireless Telegraph & Signal Company in the United Kingdom in 1897 (which became the Marconi Company). He succeeded in making a commercial success of radio by innovating and building on the work of previous experimenters and physicists. In 1929, the King of Italy ennobled Marconi as a Marchese (marquis). This came too late as Marconi felt he was let down by his own country. He felt that Italy did not take his invention seriously. Which is why he came to England where his inventions flourished. Leading up to and during the First World War, Marconi helped Britain with technology in radio communications and direction finding innovations. With the advent of radio the use of cables slowly diminished but nevertheless cables were used to communicate throughout the first and Second World Wars. Even today there are many ships that specialise in laying communication cables between remote countries to aid Internet communications and to backup satellite systems.

1. (Marconi's law) the relationship between the height of an aerial and the distance a radio signal could travel.

World War I.

The Submarine Telegraph Company was taken over by the GPO (General Post Office) in 1890 and as well as the cables, the GPO acquired the cable ship, *CS Lady Carmichael*. Renamed *CS Alert* it was used to maintain Channel cables until scrapped in 1915. In the early hours of 5 August 1914 the British Cable Ship *CS Alert* took the first significant action only a few hours after war was declared. Britain carried out something that seemed to be minor, but was actually vital. The British cable ship severed five German submarine cables which passed from Emden in north Germany, through the English Channel to Vigo, Tenerife, the Azores and the USA. This operation was a major blow, forcing Germany to use radio for international communications for the duration of the war. Having said that, Germany could communicate to the United States using the submarine cable that went via Sweden. The Swedish cable came through London's Electra House and could be intercepted by decryption staff, housed at the Admiralty's Room 40 known as NID25. (Naval Intelligence Department 25) Together with the increasing use of the new-fangled radio for communications, between military commanders and their operational units in the field, the British and French could listen in to much of the enemy's communications.

Shortly after *CS Alert's* actions in the Channel, British Naval intelligence set up Room 40 at the Admiralty to process the goldmine of information produced by eavesdropping on the enemy's communications. Much of the information was encrypted, the staff in Room 40 aimed to crack the codes. To help, they often used the associated traffic analysis to gather the information they needed. This involved looking at other elements of a communication. You can deduce a lot of information by looking at the time and duration of a message and call signs. It is also possible to ascertain the location of enemy transmitters using direction finding techniques. The intercept operator could note and identify the location of the enemy along with their ship or military unit, so it could be monitored and tracked. Trained listeners who could even detect specific enemy operators by their "fist" this is the subtle variations in the sending pattern of the Morse code, by relative duration of the dots, dashes and gaps for different letters. There was also a procedure known as radio fingerprinting to identify who was sending the message.

The Zimmerman telegram

An act of parliament was required before the Eastern Telegraph Co at Electra House could intercept diplomatic cables for the purpose of codebreaking. Admiral Reginald Hall the Director of Naval Intelligence put pressure on the Government, eventually the act was passed.

Germany believed that they could keep the USA out of the European conflict by creating a diversion by way of a war between Mexico and the United States, this was outlined in the

Zimmerman telegram. The publication of this outraged Americans, just as German U-boats started sinking American ships in the North Atlantic. US President Woodrow Wilson asked Congress for "a war to end all wars" that would "make the world safe for democracy", and Congress voted to declare war on Germany on 6th April 1917. The same day, the U.S. declared war on the Austro-Hungarian Empire.

As the United States entered into World War I in 1917 there had been after two and a half years of efforts by the President to keep America neutral. Apart from an Anglophile element supporting the British, American public opinion went along with neutrality at first. The sentiment for neutrality was strong among Irish Americans, German Americans and Swedish Americans, as well as among church leaders and women in general. On the other hand, even before World War I broke out American opinion towards Germany was already more negative than it was toward any other country in Europe. The population increasingly came to see the German Empire as the villain after news of atrocities in Belgium in 1914 and with the sinking of the Cunard passenger liner RMS Lusitania in May 1915. Wilson made all the key decisions and kept the economy on a peacetime basis, while making lucrative largescale loans to Britain and France. To preclude making any military threat President Wilson made only minimal preparations for war and kept the United States Army on its small peacetime basis, despite increasing demands for preparedness. However, he did enlarge the United States Navy.

On 17 January 1917 a telegram was received at Room 40 by Nigel de Grey who joined the Royal Naval Volunteer Reserve and served in Belgium. In early 1915 he was transferred to Naval Intelligence Division, Room 40 codebreaking section. Also with him was Codebreaker Alfred Dillwyn Knox (Dilly Knox), a British classics scholar and papyrologist from King's College, Cambridge and they were manning the Room 40 night watch at this time. The message they received was in the German diplomatic code 0075, originally this code was intercepted in November 1916. As the message was being decoded, Nigel de Grey noticed it was being sent to Mexico, via count von Bernstorf the German ambassador to the USA, and coming from the German foreign minister Arthur Zimmerman. To the codebreakers astonishment this was gold dust. Nigel de Grey grabbed the half decoded message ran down the corridor to the Director of Naval Intelligence (DNI). Admiral Reginal Hall was at his desk when the office door burst open, Nigel de Grey slammed his decrypts onto the table, "Do you want to bring America into the war, Sir?" he asked.

The Zimmerman telegram was trying to instigate a war between USA and Mexico which would be assisted by Japan and supported by Germany. The prize for Mexico would be to reclaim their lost territories. The USA for many years had been at odds with Mexico in 1845 USA won Texas as a state and in 1912 New Mexico and Arizona. To keep the USA out of the European conflict, Germany needed to maintain this aggression between the USA and Mexico. $340,000 was funded by a German secret service agent Felix A Summerfield, who operated in Mexico and the United States between 1908 and 1919. He was chief of the Mexican Secret Service under President Francisco I. The plan was to send the Zimmerman telegram by submarine along with the German 0075 code book in the diplomatic pouch, so that when it arrived was at the German Embassy in Washington the ambassador Count von Burnstorff could decipher and read it.

Cargo submarine The Deutschland was scheduled to sail on 15 January 1917 with the Zimmerman telegram. But due to a proposed plan in February 1917 that Germany would resume unrestricted submarine warfare, The Deutschland was drafted back into service and her mission was aborted. Had the Zimmerman telegram been delivered by the submarine instead of cable and not intercepted by the British the outcome would have certainly changed the course of the First World War and would possibly have changed the course of history. The concern was, would the Americans think that the Zimmerman telegram was a hoax to bring them into a war that President Woodrow Wilson did not want? Also would this cause the Germans to suspect that their cables had been intercepted and how would they react?

The route of the Zimmerman telegram

German cables were routed through neutral Sweden. What the Germans didn't know and were not to find out was that all Swedish cables routed to the USA went via Electra house in London for switch routing. By Sweden transmitting a signal from Germany to the United States this contravened Sweden's neutrality. As a result Sweden later rerouted Germany's cables via Buenos Aires, which were then retransmitted onto Washington. Burnstorff's duty was to inform Germany's minister in Mexico Heinrich von Eckardt. If Admiral Reginald Hall DNI, could obtain a copy of the Mexico message which could have a different date stamp and sent with a different cipher than that of 0075, it could possibly resolve Admiral Hall's issues. The story is that the British agent Thomas Hohler arranged for a break-in at the Mexican telegraph office. The telegram, which was supposed to be found by accident, was then passed to Room 40 for decoding. When hypothetically realising its contents Naval Intelligence alerted the US ambassador in London, just over one month after the Zimmerman telegram had been received at Room 40. The time-lapse would give credence to the story. The information in the telegram was sent to President Woodrow Wilson of the United States, who immediately realised that Germany was to become their enemy. In early 1917, Germany had decided to resume all-out submarine warfare on every commercial ship headed toward Britain, realizing that this decision would almost certainly mean war with the United States.

In 1919 due to the success of Room 40's intercepted radio and cable signals, Lord Curzon the Foreign Secretary merged two code breaking organisations together, NID 25 known as Room 40 at the Admiralty and the code breaking section at the War office known as MI1b. They were brought together under one roof and became known as the Government Code and Cypher School, (GC&CS) which during the interwar period was eventually housed at Broadway buildings 54 Broadway London SW1, close to the Foreign Office and just across the way from Westminster Abbey. The building also housed the offices of MI6 the Secret Intelligence Service. The codebreakers were controlled by the chief of MI6 Admiral Hugh Sinclair. Just prior to the Second World War the code breaking organisation moved to a safe location in northern Buckinghamshire at Bletchley Park. After World War II the Government code and Cypher School became known as Government Communications headquarters and eventually moved to their current location in Cheltenham, Gloucestershire, via a brief spell at Eastcote, Middlesex.

Courtesy GCHQ Cheltenham

Secret Intelligence Service

The Secret Intelligence Service normally known as MI6, was created in 1909 following pressure from the government and the population in an overhyped scare about German spies and agents in Britain. Britain has always had a fear of enemy spies especially since the reign of Queen Elizabeth I. In the 16th century Sir Francis Walsingham, secretary of state was appointed the Queen's spymaster. There were relentless fears of a Catholic conspiracy that Mary Queen of Scots would try to overthrow the Crown. This became a constant worry. Eventually spies were trapped and arrested when Anthony Babington's treason plot was foiled, which ultimately resulted in the execution of Mary Queen of Scots. The continued threat of foreign spies travelling across Britain from foreign lands reporting back to presumed enemies has always been in the British psyche.

The New Germany

Coming forward a few hundred years, this phenomenon has never ceased. There has always been many stories about spies or agents coming to Britain to threaten our mere existence. This was especially true at the turn of the 20th century. On January 27th 1851 the eldest child of Crown Prince Frederick of Prussia and Victoria, daughter of Queen Victoria of England, was born in Berlin. Wilhelm became Kaiser at the age of 29. Kaiser Wilhelm II initially admired the great German statesman Otto von Bismarck, known as the Iron Chancellor, who created one unified German state from many principalities within the Prussian kingdom, thereby building the modern Germany. As years passed the Kaiser didn't see eye to eye with Bismarck and ultimately forced Bismarck to resign in 1890, eight years later Bismarck died in Hamburg. Among the empires of Britain, Russia and France, Germany was the new kid on the block, wanting power and wanted it quickly. At that time, Britain ruled the most powerful empire the world had ever known and Germany wanting some of the action to match and overtake British supremacy.

Alfred Tirpitz was born in Brandenburg March 1849. He joined the Prussian Navy in 1865. On the creation of the German fleet in 1871, he joined the torpedo Squadron. After years of climbing the promotional ladder Tirpitz eventually became Secretary of State of the *Reichsmarineamt* (the Imperial naval office). He attracted the attention and support of Kaiser Wilhelm II. and was promoted to captain. Captain Tirpitz became chief of the naval staff in 1892 and rear Admiral in 1895. Tirpitz was ennobled to von Tirpitz in 1900. Tirpitz aggressively expanded the German Navy which became the second largest navy in the world, at 40% the size of the British Royal Navy. Otto von Tirpitz became Germany's Grand Admiral in 1911. Kaiser Wilhelm II continued to expand the German Empire, while his growing navy was becoming a constant threat to Britain. Also there had always been a Royal distrust between Wilhelm and his late grandmother Queen Victoria and then with Edward VII which did not help the fears and growing tension between the two nations.

With the threat of German expansion, Britain became worried with the possibility of a war with Germany, and these early rumours were blown out of proportion. The Prime Minister, Herbert Asquith, reacted to popular concern. At the turn of the century stories broke out in the newspapers, of German spies seen in the vicinity of British military bases and naval dockyards. With apparent questioning they claimed to be artists just drawing and sketching the scenery. At that time there were many Germans living in England. A popular occupation for them was the catering industry, hotels, waiters and cooks in restaurants. The government was under pressure from public opinion, which whipped into a frenzy by the press would have liked to see all German waiters rounded up and deported. Many Germans in England, if asked, would state they came from Switzerland. The British newspapers told their readers that "if a foreigner claims to come from Switzerland, they should ask to see their passport". The government was so concerned about public opinion that by December 1907 it was compelled to act.

Committee of Imperial Defence

The Committee of Imperial Defence was an important ad hoc part of the government of the United Kingdom and the British Empire from just after the Second Boer War (1902) until the start of the Second World War in 1939. It was established by Prime Minister Arthur Balfour, following the recommendations of the Elgin Committee, chaired by Lord Elgin. It was intended as an advisory committee for the Prime Minister, one that would be small and flexible; replacing the Cabinet's decaying Defence Committee, which had usually only met during periods of crisis.

The committee was responsible for research and some coordination on issues of military strategy. Typically, a temporary subcommittee would be set up to investigate and report at length on a specific topic. A large number of such subcommittees were engendered over the decades, on topics such as foreign espionage. The Committee of Imperial Defence was to create a subcommittee known as the Secret Service Bureau (SSB) headed by Rear Admiral Bethell, director of Naval Intelligence (DNI). The Secret Service Bureau was split into Home and Foreign Sections, In August 1909 Captain Mansfield Cumming [Mansfield George Smith Cumming] a 50 year-old Royal Navy officer, received a letter from Admiral Bethell.

My Dear Mansfield Cumming

Boom defence must be getting a bit stale with you and the recent experiments with Ferret rather discounts yours at Southampton. You may therefore perhaps like a new billet. If so I have something good I can offer you and if you would like to come and see me on Thursday about noon I will tell you what it is.

Yours sincerely

A E Bethell

Mansfield Cumming was working at Southampton on experimental boom defences at the time. He was chosen to lead the Foreign Section of the new service. He was an unusual choice, having neither intelligence experience nor linguistic skills, but he was apparently recommended for the role due to 'special qualifications'. He was, however, a workaholic and commenced his duties in October 1909, a week early. So it is no surprise that his diary entry for that first day stated that he "went to the office and remained [there] all day, but saw no one, nor was there anything to do there". Being Head of the foreign section of the SSB, Mansfield Cumming was none too pleased to find he would be sharing his position with his army opposite number Capt Vernon Kell. Cumming was worried that Kell could take over and he would be subordinate to Kell who was supposed to be running the home section of the service.

Kell's home section of the service became known as military office section 5. (MO5). And Mansfield Coming's section had a variety of names, (see below). Mansfield Cumming left a legacy that still exists in the organisation today. He called intelligence reports 'CX reports' – the name still employed by the Service. Also he always used a fountain pen with green ink: he signed his name with "C" which probably would have stood for Cumming. Another tradition which is still used today is that the chief of the Secret Intelligence Services, will still sign their memos and letters in green ink with the letter "C" but nowadays it refers to chief and definitely not "M" as in James Bond stories.

From 1909 and through World War 1 the Service had a variety of names including the 'Foreign Intelligence Service, the 'Secret Service', 'MI1(c)', the 'Special Intelligence Service' and even 'C's organisation'. But, around 1920, the title, Secret Intelligence Service (SIS) was adopted. This is the official title that the Service has continued to use ever since. The origins of the use of 'MI6' are to be found at the start of the Second World

War when this abbreviation was adopted as a flag of convenience. It was used extensively throughout the war, especially if an organisational link needed to be made with MI5 (the Security Service). Although 'MI6' officially fell into disuse years ago, many writers and journalists continue to use it to describe the Secret Intelligence Service. The organisation is still responsible for deploying agents in foreign lands and monitoring security threats from abroad. Whereas the term MI5 is slowly being replaced by 'The Security Service', whose agents operate from within the United Kingdom to monitor security threats at home and to maintain defence of the realm.

64 Victoria Street

Cumming's original office was at 64 Victoria Street SW1. At first the Foreign and Home Sections shared an office but Mansfield Cumming soon decided he needed his own base and one that provided him with accommodation.

Ashley Mansions.

He settled on Ashley Mansions in Vauxhall Bridge Road. In early in 1910 he set up a phoney address with the Post Office – Messrs Rasen Falcon Limited, a firm of 'shippers and exporters'. This was the first instance of what has since then become the classic 'import/export' espionage cover and anything sent to this address was forwarded to him at Ashley Mansions.

2 Whitehall Court.

In 1911 the Section again relocated, this time to No.2 Whitehall Court, near to the War Office and close proximity to the Admiralty and Foreign Office, providing more space for the growing service. During the First World War, the Service's role and its workforce grew, which led to expansion into other offices. Potential officers were interviewed and assessed at a location in Kingsway, while a 'very secret' Air Section was based in South Lambeth Road.

Following the outbreak of World War I in 1914 the Foreign Section worked more closely with Military Intelligence. In 1916 it adopted the cover name of MI1(c), still part of the War Office. In October 1914 Cumming suffered a personal tragedy. He and his son were involved in a motor car accident in France. Cumming's injuries were severe, broken legs and the loss of a foot, while his son suffered fatal head injuries. This was a period of dramatic growth and change for the Service, but its work had a major influence on the eventual victory. In November 1914 British intelligence in the Netherlands was approached by Karl Krüger, a former German naval officer. He possessed access to a wide range of information on naval construction and fleet dispositions and was willing to sell these secrets at a price. Krüger provided vital intelligence for the rest of the war including crucial revelations regarding German losses at the Battle of Jutland in 1916.

MI6 and the codebreakers

Naval intelligence department 25 (NID 25) was located in room No.40 at the Admiralty, Old buildings in London during World War I. It was the Department for breaking enemy naval and diplomatic codes, from the interception of radio signals and diplomatic telegraph cables. The department became known as Room 40 and was also responsible for a system known as traffic analysis. Room 40 was set up in 1914 by the Director of Naval Intelligence Henry Oliver and his friend Sir James Ewing, a brilliant engineer and then director of Naval Education based at Greenwich Naval College. Also supported by the first Lord of the Admiralty Winston Churchill, who became a great ambassador of signals intelligence especially later during World War II.

In its first 17 years, MI6 had been based in four different buildings around London as various senior figures had tried to establish its role. In 1926 Rear Admiral Hugh 'Quex' Sinclair, previously Director of Naval Intelligence 1919–1921 has now become the chief of the Secret Intelligence Service "C". Sinclair was also director of the codebreakers along with the operational head Commander Alistair Denniston. They eventually moved the Service and GC&CS, into Broadway Buildings, a brass plate on the entrance stated "MINIMAX FIRE EXTINGUISHER COMPANY which fooled no one, especially the London cabbies with all the comings and goings at the place. Just prior to the outbreak of the Second World War, GC&CS and a small section of MI6 including section VIII (communications) established itself at Bletchley Park in Buckinghamshire while

MI6 kept its headquarters at Broadway. It was the Service's home until 1964.

The purchase of Bletchley Park

In July 1938, Admiral Hugh Sinclair ("C") bought a large part of the Bletchley Park estate in Buckinghamshire it consisted of a Mansion house with 44 acres of land, for which he paid just £6,000. This was to become a wartime base for MI6 and GC&CS. The reasons for moving to Bletchley was that it had good communication links with London by road and rail. Also it was in close proximity to the main telephone trunk line from London to the north-west of Britain and there was plenty of room for expansion. What also became important were useful links with the big university towns of Oxford and Cambridge, by way of a railway line which linked both towns with a station at Bletchley.

After a trial run they returned to London in September 1938 prior to the Munich Crisis. In August 1939 just a few weeks before the outbreak of World War II GC&CS staff were transferred to Bletchley on a permanent basis. A 24 hour MI6 communication service with four transmitters and six receivers was set up there. Since this was the 10th radio station in an area of Buckinghamshire and Bedfordshire, it became known as station X (the Roman numeral for ten). Section D (Destruction) also moved to Bletchley in early 1939 to develop sabotage material, including incendiaries and plastic explosives. This section moved to other locations in 1941 when it became SOE (Special Operations Executive). Just after the beginning of the war in November 1939 Station X was to be dismantled, owing to the possibility of being pinpointed by enemy direction finding and therefore giving away the location of the British codebreakers. By January 1940 MI6 section VIII. (Communications) had moved 4 ½ miles west of Bletchley Park to Whaddon Hall, Buckinghamshire. This became known as special communications unit one (SCU1), run by Brigadier Richard Gambier-Parry an ex UK sales manager of the Philco Radio Company. This section communicated the majority of disseminated signal traffic (Ultra) from Bletchley Park to wherever it was needed in the European and North African theatres of war.

MI6 section VIII had another important radio intercept station at Hanslope Park just 10 miles north of Bletchley Park, also controlled by Gambier-Parry known as the Radio Security Service (RSS). It was responsible for intercepting clandestine radio signals from enemy agents attempting to operate in Britain and also signals from the *Abwehr* the German intelligence organisation operating throughout Europe. After the war Hanslope Park became the Diplomatic Wireless Service (DWS) supporting British embassies. This station still operates today as part of the Foreign & Commonwealth Office. (FCO)

The Venlo incident

Hugh Sinclair died in November 1939 and was replaced by Colonel Stewart Menzies, who had served as his deputy. Menzies took over a service comprising 42 officers and 55 secretaries. Becoming Chief just two months after war was declared, Menzies oversaw a dramatic expansion of both MI6 and GC&CS in the fight to defeat the Axis powers. November 1939 was a tough time for the Secret Intelligence Service as the MI6 organisation became associated by what became known as The Venlo Incident. MI6 was caught out big time. The Prime Minister Neville Chamberlain even after war was declared in September 1939 was still attempting to make some kind of peace with Hitler, much to the disgust of Prime Minister in waiting Winston Churchill. An MI6 network based in Holland which basically was used for shipping information between Europe and Britain was to stage a special liaison with the enemy. This was arranged with some allegedly German dissidents who wanted to see Hitler removed. In reality this was all a German sting, set up by Heinrich Himmler, Reinhard Heydrich, and Walter Schellenberg an *SS-Oberfuhrer of the Sicherhietsdienst.* (Intelligence organisation of the Gestapo). Schellenberg called himself Major Schammer and claimed that he wanted Hitler overthrown. A secret meeting was arranged with two MI6 officers Captain Sigismund Payne-Best, who was a British Army intelligence officer working on behalf of MI6 and residing in The Hague, Major Richard Henry Stevens and a Dutch intelligence officer Dirk Klopp. The meeting place was to be at the Cafe Bockus at the frontier point of the German border. It was to take place at 4 PM on 9th November 1939. The MI6 officers were told to bring documentation with them of other agents that can be contacted. Most MI6 agents were disguised as British passport control officers at British embassies. This fooled no one as apparently everybody knew this. It was no secret at all and a very dangerous oversight.

Armed with all this information a car took the MI6 officers to the arranged meeting. Once they arrived at the German border the car stopped at the barrier. The *SS-Sonderkomandos* were waiting. They suddenly pounced on the car and there was a gun battle in which Dirk Klopp, was fatally wounded. They dragged the car over the border into the German territory then Stevens and Best were kidnapped. They were taken to Düsseldorf where they were interrogated by the SS and then spent the rest of the war in several concentration camps. This was a great success for Germany as Best and Payne had on their person all the details of all the MI6 agents, addresses, places of work and hideouts. So in one afternoon the whole of MI6 in Europe collapsed and many agents were arrested. Another interesting fact was that prior to this the German scam involved setting up a two-way radio link with MI6 to pass on information. This radio station was still live and broadcasting information to the Germans for nine days after the Venlo incident. Captain Payne and Major Stevens miraculously survived the war and were released in 1945.

Claude Dansey

Was recruited by MI5 during World War I and put in charge of port intelligence, surveillance and monitoring civilian passengers at ports. During World War II he was assigned as chief of the MI6 station in Rome as a passport control officer at the British Embassy. He predicted that sooner or later MI6 would be heading for a disaster. As a businessman before the war he had many contacts throughout Europe. Dansey foresaw that MI6 would drop itself in the mire, so he took it upon himself to setup a parallel organisation. This was based at Bush House in London and operated under the cover of an import export organisation Geoffrey Duveen & company

His MI6 codename was Z. So he formed the Z organisation. He hired over 200 executives who would spy on behalf of Britain. They would do this on a voluntary basis for the sheer thrill of espionage. They were not allowed to take risks, they didn't write anything down or take photographs and everything they did was to be committed to memory. When push came to shove in 1939, once MI6 lost its organisation through the Venlo incident, Claude Dansey's Z organisation took over MI6's operations. You could say it saved the country's intelligence service. Dancy was never rewarded for setting up his parallel organisation to MI6. Part of the reason was that he was never liked and in fact most people hated him as he was aggressive and rude. By all accounts not a nice person. By 1945 it appeared that Dansey had outlived his usefulness and he was assigned to meaningless duties. He got bored and resigned, dying just three years later in

1947 of heart disease. Only a few friends of the Z organisation attended the funeral.

MI6 eventually recovered from the Venlo incident and operated successfully throughout the rest of the war. By the beginning of 1944, 837 people worked at their headquarters. Menzies had played an important role in the 'secret war', keeping his position when many around him lost theirs. MI6 still operates today though the name is now defunct. The Secret Intelligence Service headquarters are based in London. Their offices which are officially known as VX also sometimes called the 'green building' which is located at Vauxhall Cross, 85 Albert Embankment, on the south bank of the River Thames. The building has been the headquarters of the SIS since 1994.

List of other military intelligence sections.

Most of them are now defunct or have been renamed.

MI1a: Distribution of reports, intelligence records.

MI1b: Interception and cryptanalysis.

MI1c: The Secret Service/SIS.

MI1d: Communications security.

MI1e: Wireless telegraphy.

MI1f: Personnel and finance.

MI1g: Security, deception and counter intelligence

More military intelligence sections categories to change with time.

MI1 Codes and cyphers. Later merged with other codebreaking agencies and became Government Code and Cypher School (now known as Government Communications Headquarters).

MI2 Information on Middle and Far East, Scandinavia, US, USSR, Central and South America.

MI3 Information on Eastern Europe and the Baltic Provinces (plus USSR and Scandinavia after summer 1941).

MI4 Geographical section—maps (transferred to Military Operations in April 1940).

MI5 Counterintelligence. To become the security service.

MI6 Liaison with Secret Intelligence Service and Foreign Office.

MI7 Press and propaganda (transferred to Ministry of Information in May 1940).

MI8 Signals interception and communications security.

MI9 Escaped British PoW debriefing, escape and evasion (also: enemy PoW interrogation until 1941).

MI10 Technical Intelligence worldwide.

MI11 Military Security.

MI12 Liaison with censorship organisations in Ministry of Information, military censorship.

MI13   Undocumented Intelligence and Special operations

MI14   Germany and German occupied territories (aerial photography until Spring 1943).

MI15   Aerial photography. In the Spring of 1943, aerial photography moved to the Air Ministry and MI15 becoming Air Defence Intelligence.

MI16   Scientific Intelligence (formed 1945).[5]

MI17   Secretariat for Director of Military Intelligence from April 1943.

MI18   Officially used only in fiction. In theory (with little evidence) to have been responsible for identifying and destroying communist organisation in German occupied territory and attempting slow the Soviet advance in order to ensure the allies reached Berlin before the Soviets. May also have assisted with the American efforts to recruit and capturing axis defectors and prevent them from defecting or being captured by the USSR.

MI19   Enemy prisoner of war interrogation (formed from MI9 in December 1941).

MI (JIS)   Related to Joint Intelligence Staff, a subgroup of the Joint Intelligence Committee.

            Axis planning staff.

MI L(R)   Russian Liaison.

Operation Mincemeat

Just as Operation Overlord, in June 1944, (D Day) was a divisionary plan, or deception, where the Allies duped Hitler into believing the main invasion was to be at Pas de Calais, when the true invasion was, as we now know, on the Normandy beaches. Operation Mincemeat, in 1943, was just a part of the deception to once again deceive the Germans into misbelief

The story starts in North Africa and takes us to London, Spain, Germany, Cairo, Greece, and ends up in Sicily, as Operation Husky.

In November 1942, Field Marshal Rommel was having a hard time in North Africa. His Africa corps was being shunted back and forth, with successes and failures like those of the British eighth army. The Allies are now getting the upper hand.

The unwell Erwin Rommel had a major problem with his diminishing supply lines, owing to the success of Bletchley Park's interception of Italian supply ship codes, from the Enigma & Haglin cypher machines, which the Italian navy were using.

Rommel's supplies were being delivered to North Africa's ports and thanks to Ultra, (Bletchley Park's disseminated codes) the Royal Navy and the Royal Air Force were destroying his supply lines. In October and November 1942, the second battle of El Alamein was testament to Rommel's retreat. Roosevelt agrees with Churchill that we now needed to attack the "soft underbelly of Europe" to rid Italy of the Nazis. Churchill tells Roosevelt "any damn fool" will realise that Sicily would be the Allies obvious next move. We need a very good deception plan. The seeds of a major deception were well and truly planted. The plan was to make the Germans believe that the Allies would invade Corsica, Sardinia and especially Greece which will give access through the Balkans to Italy. The British basis in Alexandria and Cairo were hotbeds of spies. Information would get to the Italians at breakneck speed via foreign agents and prostitutes. To start the deception, British troops were sent into towns to buy up Greek phrasebooks and maps of Greek towns. Also, anything to do with Greek customs. But much more than this was needed to fool the Germans.

Back in 1941, Winston Churchill instigated what was known as the London Control Section (LCS) this was a committee of top-ranking military officers that would plan deception campaigns. They would meet at the cabinet War Room beneath the Foreign Office.

The committee was chaired by Col. John Bevan, an expert in deception planning. Bevan had a colleague in Cairo doing a similar job. Dudley Clark was with A Force, planning deception operations for the North Africa Campagne. It was decided that the plan for this operation was to be called Operation Barclay. Two members of the committee were given a part of the plan to work on.

Connection at the Admiralty

Admiral John Godfrey was the Director of Naval Intelligence. Produced what is known as the Trout memo it was passed to his assistant, Commander Ian Fleming, of James Bond fame. Fleming who worked in room 39 of the Admiralty building was a great lover of mystery and adventure books. One day, he read a book called "The Milliner's Hat Mystery" by Sir Basil Thomson. Thomson was with the Metropolitan Police and worked closely with MI5. The book involved the story of a body being found in a barn. The body had a hat beside it that contained some secret plans, which turned out to be fake. The story intrigued Fleming, as his job involved cooking up covert plans and undercover operations (see "Operation Ruthless" in Journey to station X). Admiral Godfrey's trout memo was a similar ruse. Fleming worked in close liaison with Room 13 in the basement at the Admiralty building. They worked on putting some of Fleming's plans into action. One of the members of Room 13 department 17M was Ewen Montagu. Prior to the war Montagu was a barrister. As war broke out he was requisitioned into the Naval Intelligence Department at the Admiralty.

Fleming's plan

"Plan No 28, not a very nice one. Obtain a body, make sure it's a fresh one. Hide some fake plans on it and leave it where the enemy will find it."

Ewen Montagu would have known of Fleming's plan. Montagu was one of the members at the LCS. Another member of LCS was an RAF officer by the name of Charles Cholmondeley, a bit of a whiz kid, who liked fast cars and excitement. Cholmondeley was requisitioned to work with MI5 and found himself working on the same committee at the LCS with Montagu. At an LCS meeting, Operation Barclay was being discussed. Fleming's Plan 28 would have been deliberated. Bevan and the committee decided that Plan 28 should be investigated as a possible part of Operation Barclay. Ewen Montagu and Charles Cholmondeley were given the job. The job that was to involve obtaining a body, lacing it with fake plans, and placing it where the enemy would find it. This plan needed an operational name, and this was done by applying to the admiralty for the next name on the list of military operations. Just by luck, the next on the list was an appropriate one. "Operation Mincemeat"

Locate a body

Prior to the war, as a lawyer, Montagu got to know people in certain areas of importance like a top government pathologist Sir Bernard Spillsbury. Montague approached Spillsbury to enquire which type of body would be required, as it had to be one that would convincingly deceive the enemy. It was thought that a poison case would be the answer, as some poisons are difficult to detect and identify after a time.

Cholmondeley and Montagu came up with a plan that a body would be thrown with a parachute out of an aircraft over Spain, as if the crew had bailed out from a troubled aircraft. It was established that the authorities would conduct a post-mortem and would soon realise that the body was dead before it hit the ground. A better idea was to drop the body over the side of a submarine, and let the current of the sea wash it up on the beach where it could be found. Possibly off the coast of Spain.

Obtain a body

You would think in wartime that it would be relatively easy to obtain a body, what with the bombing, and the Blitz. The problem was to find the right type of body. How did it die? What is its age? What are the injuries? Then, how do you explain to the relatives that their loved one's body is required for secret government work?

A different approach was needed, so a visit was made to a man who had in his possession no shortage of dead bodies of every shape and size. This was Sir Bentley-Purchase, the coroner of St Pancras. So a visit was made to keep an eye out for the right sort of body. Youngish, deadish and well poisoned. A few days later, the phone rang in Ewen Montagu's office, it was Bentley-Purchase. The voice on the end of the line called out "Montagu, I've got one for you! You had better be quick, it's in the fridge!"

Cholmondeley and Montagu hastily made their way to St Pancras morgue, to inspect the body. Bentley-Purchase explained that this poor fellow was apparently a vagrant, who it is understood originally made his way from Wales to London, where he probably believed that the streets were paved with gold. He either committed suicide by taking rat poison, or he accidentally poisoned himself by scavenging food from dustbins. Bentley-Purchase explained that it is unlikely that a

Spanish pathologist would be able to detect Warfarin in the blood after the body had been immersed in seawater for some time. It was now also established that the body had a name, Glyndwyr Michael, and his entry in the Register of death states that he "was a lunatic and died by suicide from phosphorus poison". Glyndwr Michael born at 136 Commercial Street, Aberbargoed Wales on 4th Jan 1909

Due to severe unemployment Glyndwr Michael's father Thomas Michael committed suicide. Glyndwr believed things were hopeless in Aberbargoed, no work, no food and a life of poverty. He decided to make his way to London in the hope of a better life.

Bring the body back to life

The plan was now to create a suitable character to deliver notional secret plans to the Germans without alerting them of the hoax. Somehow the enemy needs to know that the next target for the British and Americans in North Africa will be Greece and not the obvious one, Sicily. But at the same time the Germans would know that every battle throughout history has at least three basic principles: a plan, a surprise attack and a diversion or a deception. Therefore we must make the Germans think that Sicily is a deception plan. Wow! That will take some doing.

Back to our body: He would need a name and a rank, and a character. Major William Martin, temporary captain, was brought to life. He is going to be our messenger. A visit to Gieves & Hawkes, bespoke uniform tailors of Saville Row, was made by Cholmondeley to purchase a battle dress uniform, made to measure without actually seeing the client, and of course the tailors were sworn to secrecy. Owing to rationing certain clothes were very hard to come by, undergarments for Major Martin were sourced from a deceased warden of New College Oxford, whose collection of undies was second-to-none. Once all the appropriate clothes were obtained, a visit was paid to Major Martin's temporary home at the St Pancras cooler. He was rather stiff, nevertheless the clothes had to go on. Except for the boots, that would be done later. Montagu and Cholmondeley then gave Major Martin a personality by means of putting stuff into his pockets and wallet., It is possible that they put far too much clutter into the Major's pockets! As the Germans may have believed that there were just too many clues. Especially stubs from theatre tickets which were dated just two days prior the alleged aircraft crash, so the thoughts were Major Martin could have only got to Spain by aircraft.

So here follows the list of pocket litter placed on our Major: Bus tickets; loose change; keys on a key ring, an intentionally out-of-date naval ID card, a love letter from his fiancée, Pam: cigarettes, matches, a letter from Lloyds Bank, stating that he is overdrawn, a photo of Pam, which was actually a holiday snap of an MI5 secretary, Jean Leslie; a receipt for an engagement ring, £53.6s 0p from SJ Philips of Bond Street. And not forgetting the theatre ticket stubs. Now the main crux, the deception. Major Martin is to deliver three important letters to three important people. The letters are from two important people, the letters are real. The people are real, but it's all part of the hoax. The letters have to be very subtle, they would obviously not say "Dear Commander, we will be invading Greece tomorrow at 1100 hours". If that was so, the Germans would be waiting for us in Sicily without a doubt. The first letter was from Lieutenant General Sir Archibald Nye to General Alexander, the head of 18th Army Group Cairo. The next letter was from Louis Mountbatten to commander in charge of the Eastern Mediterranean Fleet Admiral Andrew Cunningham. The final letter was from Mountbatten, to US General Eisenhower.

The letters were very carefully designed by the LCS, and the Wireless Board (Department which fabricated fictitious information for our double-cross agents). There were many rewrites and meetings and debates about the content. Once it was decided upon, Mountbatten and Lt General Nye rewrote the letters in their own style, using the predetermined information. Once the scripts were agreed upon, they were typed on the correct typewriters for that department on the relevant stationery, including being signed in the correct inks by the right people, Mountbatten and Nye, for ultimate authenticity.

The letters were then sent to a forensics laboratory to be photographed and have some special microscopic features added to them, along with careful folds in the papers, for future detection. The letters were placed into envelopes, sealed and put into Major Martin's briefcase. The letters were embossed with authorized wax seals to be placed in an official government leather briefcase and locked. The key was put on Major Martin's keyring.

Spain

It has been decided to send Major Martin to Spain by submarine. Spain declared neutrality during WWII, but in reality the Spanish were leaning heavily towards the Germans. You could say that Spain was a non-belligerent enemy. Spanish cities were a hotbed of German spies. The coastal areas especially were keeping a close watch on the Allied shipping. The German intelligence organisation responsible for espionage known as the *Abwehr*, were recruiting Spaniards to send any information to them for cash. So this became a very lucrative way to make some money. The Fascist dictator of Spain, Francisco Franco, only met Adolf Hitler on one occasion, on October 23rd 1940. Hitler thought Franco was a bit crazy. In charge of the *Abwehr* in Spain was Major Karl Erich Kuhlenthal, who was answerable to the Commander of the *Abwehr* in Berlin, Admiral Wilhelm Canaris. However, in the west of Spain, the *Abwehr* was closely controlled by Adolf Clauss, also known as the Shadow. Anything untoward would be reported to him then he would be there like a shot. Therefore it was decided that Major William Martin should be found in his region.

It is important that an area of the Atlantic coast line off Spain was found, so that if a body was placed in the sea it would drift in towards the coast and not get washed out to sea. The Royal Navy's hydrographic department became involved. They were the experts of trade winds, sea currents and tides. They advised Montagu that an area of the coast of Western Spain close to the fishing town of Huelva would be ideal.

Captain Bill Jewell, a Royal Naval submarine commander was briefed with this Top Secret plan. Only his officers would later be told of this mission. His submarine *HMS Seraph* was on standby at Blythe in the north east of England. She will now make her way to Holy Loch north of Greenock on the Firth of Clyde to prepare for her mission.

Prepare Major Martin

A special canister was prepared to take Major Martin's body. Up until now he has been dressed in his uniform and kept in the cooler at St Pancras. To keep his body from decomposing, dry ice will be packed into his transportation canister, his briefcase is ready with the important documents, which will be attached to him later with a leather-covered chain so that they stay together when Major Martin is found.

Ready for action

Glyndwyr Michael, a man with nothing to his name other than a life of misery ended with a nasty poisonous death, will now with his new name embark on one of the most important phases of the war: a major part of a deception that, if it works will lead the Allies into "the soft underbelly of Europe", putting the first major cracks into Hitler's so called Thousand Year Reich.

On the 17th April 1943, Major William Martin of the Royal Marines was brought to life. He was removed from the cooler, had his boots put on (with great difficulty as his feet were frozen solid and had to be defrosted with an electric heater "a nasty business"). Then he was placed in his canister with dry ice and sealed in, then to be loaded into a Fordson van. The van was to be driven by a racing driver who in wartime was working for the government on special transport assignments. John [Jock] Horsfall was more used to racing Aston Martin rally cars than Fordson vans!

At midnight on 18th April, Montagu, Cholmondeley and Horsfall loaded Major Martin in his canister and onto the van. The briefcase with the important documents were carried separately. The van left London in the early hours of the morning at high speed. Racing through red traffic lights as they sped along the Great North Road. Jock Horsfall would straighten out any bends in the road by cutting straight across from one side of the road to the other. Even today this journey could take at least nine hours on modern roads. Halfway through the journey, they stopped for a flask of tea and sandwiches. They also took a moment to take some photographs of each other. There is one photo of Jock Horsfall sitting on Major Martin's canister. They soon continued their high-speed run to Greenock.

On April 18th at mid-morning, the Fordson van was cleared through the security gates at Greenock. After some confusion, some ropes were acquired as the canister had to be lowered onto a motor launch, to be taken to *HMS Forth* waiting across the River Clyde at Holy Loch. A crane would be used to winch the canister onto the waiting submarine *HMS Seraph*. Major Martin's sea voyage was about to begin. As Cholmondeley and Montagu watched by the dock side, realising what they had created, and with a little sadness wondered whether the Germans would be taken in by the hoax.

As the launch crossed the Firth of Clyde, it approached Holy Loch where the canister was winched from *HMS Forth*, then lowered onto *HMS Seraph*. Captain Bill Jewell was handed the briefcase. He then had a meeting with his senior officers, and briefed them on the operation. The able seamen on-board *HMS Seraph* were told that the canister contained secret meteorological equipment. Once Major Martin's container was loaded via the submarine's torpedo hatch, Captain Jewell made his preparations to set sail.

HMS Seraph arrived off the coast of Huelva on 30th April 1943. Before she emerged to the surface, Captain Jewell checked his periscope. It was early morning and still dark, but he could see the glimmering lanterns all around on the small fishing boats from the town of Punta Umbria. *HMS Seraph* had to lie low until the fishing boats had caught their catch and returned to port. Eventually, the lights disappeared. *HMS Seraph* surfaced and the officers opened the torpedo loading hatch and jiggled this awkward canister out of the torpedo rack and through the hatch. Once on the deck, the officers struggled to undo the catch on the canister, but eventually it opened. Major Martin was ready to go, his briefcase was attached to his belt, his body was lifted up and thrown over the side, along with an upturned dinghy to give the impression that his aircraft had crashed, and he was unable to board the dingy owing to the briefcase connected to him.

Captain Bill Jewell and his officers read Psalm 39 to give Major Martin a send-off. They then threw the canister into the sea, which refused to sink! After some tense moments, and a few bullets fired into it, the canister filled with seawater and sank. They went back below and *HMS Seraph* pulled away. As far as Captain Bill Jewell was concerned, it was mission accomplished. Major Martin with his briefcase with those so important documents, are now drifting with an upturned dinghy off the fishing port, Punta Umbria,

A fisherman by the name of Jose Antonio Rey Maria was just returning to Punta Umbria when he noticed a body floating, face-down in the sea. After great difficulty he managed to bring the body to the beach. He called some friends and very soon there was a whole commotion. As word got around, the police were called, Major Martin had arrived. His body was taken along with his briefcase to the local mortuary. As Major Martin was in a uniform of the Royal Marines, the Spanish Navy were informed. Word also got to the local *Abwehr*, who soon were making enquiries. They wanted to know about the briefcase and where it was. When they arrived at the mortuary, the briefcase had already been collected by the Spanish Navy. Soon Adolf Clauss had been alerted by a *Abwehr* agent. An autopsy was performed the next day by Eduardo Del Torno. Major Martin was now becoming quite decomposed, and the odour on this hot day had become unbearable. Luckily, the pathologist spent very little time with our Major, and the verdict was death by drowning in sea water. The last thing that the British wanted was Major Martin with his case and all his gizmos to be bagged up and sent back to Britain without the Germans viewing the contents of the case. A funeral was arranged for 2nd May at Huelva. In attendance was British Vice Consul Francis Haselden. Martin was given a full military send-off.

But in the background, Adolf Clauss was watching. He contacted the police as he heard that the briefcase had gone missing. He was told that it was taken away along with all the junk in Major Martin's pockets by the Spanish Navy. Clauss approached the navy, who told him to go away as he had no authority: although Spain unofficially supported the Germans, the navy would not obey the *Abwehr*. Clauss realised the importance of the situation and contacted the most senior *Abwehr* officer in Madrid, Major Karl Erich Kuhlenthal. Kuhlenthal sent a signal to Berlin to the head of the *Abwehr*, explaining the full circumstances of the Major Martin situation. This signal sent by the *Abwehr* was intercepted and decoded at Bletchley Park. Once fully translated, it was sent to British Naval Intelligence.

Montagu was ecstatic that the Germans were now involved but they still had not seen the contents of the briefcase. MI5 and the LCS (London Control Section) knew that certain telephone lines to our embassy in Spain were being hacked by the Spanish on behalf of the *Abwehr*, which was very useful, as MI5 arranged to send the following message to the British Consulate who was privy to Operation Mincemeat. "Major Martin's briefcase must be found urgently unopened and

returned to London via the diplomatic bag as soon as possible"
The Times Newspaper added Major Martin's name to the
obituary column "RNVR Royal Marines – T/capt (A major)
Martin" MI5 knew that the Germans always read British
newspapers.

Admiral Wilhelm Canaris, the Commander in Chief of the
Abwehr flashed a message to the highest authorities in Spain to
locate the briefcase and hand it over immediately to the German
authorities. The brief case had now gone missing, which worried
the Germans and the British. Eventually, the briefcase was found
at the main Government offices in Madrid. The Germans
demanded that the case was handed over. They were only given
a few hours to inspect it, and it was then returned to the Spanish
authorities who sent all of Major Martin's possessions including
the briefcase back to London via the British embassy's black
diplomatic bag.

Department 17M located at Room 13 at the Admiralty was on
tenterhooks. Montagu and Cholmondeley were waiting
desperately for any news. Had the Germans seen the contents?
Had they believed the letters were genuine? Would the Germans
react to the information? These were the worrying questions that
everyone in Room 13 was sweating on. The briefcase and letters
finally arrived back at the Admiralty. They were immediately
taken to the laboratory where forensic scientists were on
standby. The briefcase was opened and the contents were
scrutinised. The envelopes were still sealed with the official
government wax seal. Initially this looked like bad news as the
letters had not been opened. The fear was that they may not have

been read by the Germans and the whole operation was a failure. But when the results came back from the laboratory, it was a different story. The envelopes were sealed, but a microscopic investigation showed that the letters had been carefully removed from the other end of the envelope by a special technique using a fine tool to roll up the letter and extract it. The microscopic folds in the letter showed it had been opened and refolded and reinserted into the envelope. This had been the case with all three letters. So the possibility was that the Germans had seen the contents of the documents but would they believe them? We could only hope.

Meanwhile, at Bletchley Park, *Abwehr* intercepted signals had been deciphered stating that important enemy documents had been retrieved and were to be taken by hand to the *fremde here der Wehrmacht*. (Foreign armies intelligence service FHW) who immediately made copies of the letters. The head at the FHW Lt Colonel Von Roenne, took them personally to the *Oberkommando der Wehrmacht* and to the desk of Adolf Hitler. As the scientific analysis was received along with the Ultra information from Bletchley Park, there were jubilations in Room 13. Cheers could be heard throughout the winding corridors in the basement at the Admiralty. Ewen Montagu immediately picked up the scrambler phone and send a message to Winston Churchill who happened to be in Canada at the time. The message read "from Montagu/Admiralty/London.-Mincemeat swallowed whole"

But the question remained did the Germans believe it, or did they see it as a hoax? The danger with any deception plan is that if the enemy realises it was a trick, they would recognise that the opposite was true. This could prove a disaster for the Allies. The whole plan was to make the Germans believe that our attack of the soft underbelly of Europe which they expected would come from Greece and Sardinia and not from the obvious Sicily.

Luckily, Hitler believed every word of it, even though his generals were not so sure. As a result of Operation Mincemeat, which was a major part of the overall deception plan of Operation Barclay, the Germans moved ten complete Panzer divisions to the Balkans. Fleets of R Boats and U Boats were sent to the Adriatic and the Eastern Mediterranean. Thousands of troops were sent to Corsica and Sardinia this was another part of the deception known called Operation Brimstone. On the 10th July 1943. American and British troops invaded Sicily in what was called Operation Husky. But through operation Barclay and our network of double agents, we made the Germans believe that invading Sicily was a bluff. But it of course was the real thing and there was virtually no opposition to Operation Husky the invasion of Sicily resulting with extremely few casualties. In other words a complete success.

Like most stories, there are conspiracy theories. It has been suggested that Major William Martin was not Glyndwyr Michael after all. It has been said in recently that Montagu and Cholmondeley swapped over the bodies at the last moment for a fresher corpse due to the excess of decomposition, to a sailor who perished on the ship *HMS Dasher*. This was a converted aircraft carrier that sank after an engine room fire on-board on

27th March 1943 near the entrance to the River Clyde. The event of this sinking was kept highly secret the belief was that it may have been struck by a torpedo from a U-boat. Although anything is possible, owing to the timing and the immense preparations that were made it seems uncertain. It is important to note that this whole affair was recorded in the book by Ewen Montagu "The Man Who Never Was" the book was based on the Admiralty reports. The question is did Montagu keep some of the details to himself? The answer is simple, we will probably never know.

However, these are the facts that we have to hand which come from the archives and Ewen Montagu's book. Is it possible that the man who never was, was in fact someone else? But at the end of the day it is the result that matters, the success of Operation Husky. The gravestone of Major Martin in Huelva was amended after the war to "Glyndwyr Michael served as Major William Martin RN".

This was the first step into the long haul into the downfall of Adolf Hitler. To use Winston Churchill's own words from late 1942 "This was [certainly] the end of the beginning"

Agent Zig Zag the spy who loved himself

This is a story about Edward Arnold Chapman. He became known as agent Zig Zag. There is a film called the Triple Cross (1966) released by Warner Bros.-Seven Arts, which tells the story of Eddie Chapman, but I believe his story is far more interesting than the film portrayed. After all in 1966 most of Eddie Chapman's activities were still covered by the 30 year rule and many of his activities remain secret until recently.

It all started in 1914. Eddie Chapman was born in Burnopfield a tiny village in Durham's coal fields. Like any other boy he was predominantly naughty, played in the streets, got up to mischief. His father was a marine engineer in the First World War who in later life ran a pub in Durham. When Eddie left school employment was virtually non-existent and he worked in a shipyard for a time before joining the army. He was eventually stationed with the Coldstream Guards at the Tower of London. Eddie enjoyed being in London especially the off duty life. He would go into London's West End and meet women and make many friends in the Soho area. This part of London is well known for nightclubs, coffee bars, dodgy dealings, not to mention ladies of the night. (Especially during the day)

It wasn't long before Eddie was getting himself into mischief with women. He was also getting into trouble with the army because he became absent without leave. In fact he decided not to go back at all. Eventually he was arrested and sent to an

Army prison for 84 days. After completing his sentence he was dishonourably discharged from the Coldstream Guards. Eddie Chapman rented a room in Shepherd's Bush West London where he met Freda Stevenson and fell in love. But this never stopped Eddie from exploring the streets of Soho making bad company and visiting bad women. He became involved with petty crimes; breaking and entering, stealing, getting involved with shady dealings including blackmail and fraud and was eventually arrested, charged and sentenced to three months in Wandsworth Prison. In prison he made friends, the wrong sort. When Eddie Chapman came out of prison, he became involved with bank robbers becoming an expert in blowing safes. In fact he enjoyed blowing things up, he didn't even do it for the money but for sheer thrill.

He was still in Soho when he met Vera Friedberg a Jewish refugee who wanted British citizenship, so as a favour they married for convenience, probably also for money even though he was he was still engaged to Freda Stevenson. Freda Stevenson became pregnant and had a baby by Eddie named Diane. Chapman was still keeping bad company getting involved with London's most notorious criminals known as the Gellie gang. They would break into banks, Eddie Chapman would use his skills to place gelignite around the lock of the banks safe. He then would get to a safe distance. There would be an almighty bang, this would normally blow the safe door right off and blow out the bank's windows at the same time. They would grab as much money as they possibly could and run for it before the police turned up.

Eddie, still engaged Freda, divorces Vera, and falls in love with Betty Farmer. One day he was involved with a break-in at the Edinburgh Co-op. He blew the safe and stole £476 3s 10d. He was arrested by the police and placed on bail. He then jumped bail and travelled to the Channel Islands with his girlfriend Betty Farmer.

On 13th February 1939 while in Jersey he booked into the Hotel de la Plage in St Helier. Chapman and his girlfriend Betty were having a nice quiet drink in the hotel, when he noticed the police coming in through the front entrance. Eddie Chapman took no chances. He flew up from his seat and made a quick exit straight through a rear window which happened to be closed at the time, smashing the glass as he jumped. He then ran down the beach and hid, leaving Betty wondering what had happened. They never saw each other again until many years later.

When nightfall came he crept into the town and booked in at a local bed and breakfast. The landlady Mrs Corfield was suspicious of him, and asked him for the money upfront. Chapman said "I'm just popping out to get some money". As there were no ATMs in those days he went across the town, broke into a nightclub entered the manager's office and emptied the safe of £25 then made his way back to the bed and breakfast, but as he entered his room the landlady alerted the police. Eddie Chapman was arrested. He went to court and was sentenced to 2 years imprisonment for this misdemeanour on the island of Jersey. This prison sentence did him a big favour, because had the mainland police caught up with Chapman he would have been taken back to England and probably faced 14 years in prison for his bank robbery escapades.

While in prison Eddie Chapman was on his best behaviour. He earned himself a trusted position, regularly cleaning the governor's house, his car and do the gardening. Charming Eddie Chapman was playing good as gold. In July 1939 on a day when the governor went out to a function. Eddie stole some cash then helped himself to the governor's bicycle and made a getaway. Eddie Chapman broke into a school and hid for the night. He stole a raincoat he found. The next day he hailed a taxi and asked to be taken to a quarry where he broke into the site office and stole 26 sticks of gelignite with a box of detonators. On 6 July 1939 he was walking along the seafront going back towards the town passing people who were sunbathing, swimming and playing football on the beach, when an off duty policeman recognised him and tried to stop him. A fight broke out. The men playing football helped the policeman to bring Chapman to the ground and pin him down. They held Chapman down, with one of the footballers sitting on top of him until the police arrived. No one realised he was carrying enough dynamite and detonators to blow half the beach up. With less than 24 hours of freedom, Eddie Chapman is locked in the back of a black Mariah being taken to St Helier police station. Eddie Chapman ends up in court once again where he is charged and found guilty and is sentenced with a further year on his prison sentence, now he is having to spend three years in a Jersey gaol. There were no more trusted positions for him that was for sure, but he did behave himself. He made a friend in prison a local hairdresser, Anthony Faramus. They planned that one day when released from prison they would go into business together and open a barbershop.

As time goes by with Chapman in prison the world is changing. The year is 1940, Britain has been at war eight months. In May Hitler invaded France and on the 29 June 1940 the Germans took over the Channel Islands. When Eddie Chapman was finally released from prison with his friend Anthony Faramus it's a very different world. The Germans are everywhere. But life is continuing as normal as it could be. Chapman and Faramus form a partnership and open a barbershop. The customers were mainly German soldiers who Chapman would joke with and pick up bits of German and try to speak the language.

One day Chapman was cycling down the road not thinking where he was going and he crashes into a German officer's dispatch motorcycle. Chapman was immediately summoned to the police station where he was interviewed by a German officer. Chapman was charged with riding a bicycle in a dangerous manner and being in possession of guns which was very illegal. Chapman never had any guns and this was the first time in his life that he had been charged with something he never actually did. He got away with a severe warning.

Chapman wasn't very happy about the situation and was becoming home sick and missing Betty, so he devised a plan of how to get back to England. But if he got back to England he might be caught by the police, so he came up with an idea. He would ask the Germans if he could become an agent and spy on their behalf. He could be taken to England secretly by boat and dropped off in a small cove somewhere and he would operate for the Germans and send secret information back. So he went to see the most senior officer at the German headquarters in Jersey, General Otto von Stulpnagel. The general listened to him, made some notes and said he would be in touch at a future date. He then returned to his work at the barbershop. Chapman and Faramus lived above the shop in some tiny rooms. One night they were awoken by the smashing down the door. The Gestapo entered the bedroom and arrested both men. They were handcuffed and dragged out of the building and driven down to the harbour. With just night clothes they were put on a small motor launch which took off at speed to arrive at the French coast. Once there, a vehicle picked them up and took them to a Gestapo prison at Romainville just outside Paris. Chapman and Faramus were given prison clothes and were told they were being charged with spying, which they obviously hadn't. Once again Chapman was charged with something he had not done and could not make out why the Germans did this to them. Faramus and Chapman were then thrown in a cell with just a straw bed.

Romainville Prison

Romainville Prison could be truly described as a hellhole. Dirty, damp, disgusting. Food was disgusting and at bare minimum. Torture was the word of the day and executions were happening all the time. The Gestapo would take revenge on anybody anywhere who would attack a German officer. They would just take a dozen or so prisoners from one of the cells and execute them in the yard. If ever there was a place waiting for Godot this was it. But Eddie Chapman made the most of everything he did. There was times when the prisoners were let out the cells for short periods. Eddie started chatting up the women prisoners and making friends. Anthony Faramus was also locked in an adjacent cell. They were given no rhyme or reason why they were there except they were told they would be charged with spying. Every day more people would be locked up and every day more people would be taken for execution. Faramus was treated exceptionally badly. On one occasion Chapman was put into solitary confinement for breaking into a woman's cell and staying there for the night. His solitary confinement was freezing cold at night. The only way Chapman could stop himself freezing to death was by covering himself with a pile of gravel that was in the corner of the cell. One day Eddie was taken out of the cell and dragged into an interview room. Eddie believed he was going to be tortured or killed.

The interview was conducted by a member of the German defence agency the *Abwehr*. The smart man in civilian clothes said his name was Dr Gruamann he started by asking questions about Chapman's past. What he thought of England and then asked him why he would like to spy for Germany. It seemed that after a long period following his original request to spy for Germany, that his request had been finally recognised. Chapman gave all the reasons that he hated Britain, because the police were after him and if he should return to Britain and caught he will face many years in prison. The *Abwehr* officer said that would be all for now. Chapman was dragged back to his cell and thrown in and the door locked behind him.

A few weeks passed before Chapman again was removed from his cell to another interview with the *Abwehr* officer. He was to be issued with his release papers, some clothes and told he would be going for training at their training centre outside Paris. Chapman was asked if he was prepared to do this. Well of course he was but he did ask for one favour, could his friend Anthony Faramus be looked after. The *Abwehr* officer told Chapman he would see what he could do but he couldn't promise anything. He was led out the prison with an armed guard. He got into a motorcar they were taken to Gare Austerlitz in Paris. The armed guard and Chapman entered the first-class compartment of a train. As the train departed Chapman and his guard enjoyed a first-class meal followed by wine. The train eventually arrived at the industrial port of Nantes on the west coast of France. They were then met by another armed guard and Chapman was put into a German staff car and taken to Villa de la Bretoniere.

Villa de la Bretoniere

Villa de la Bretoniere was a beautiful villa set in acres of its own grounds. it was once home to a wealthy Jewish businessman and his family who were thrown out when the Germans moved in. In 1940 it became an *Abwehr* training centre. To Chapman it looked like a palace. Chapman was taken inside the house where he was told to wait. He was then to be interviewed one again by Dr Graumann. This was to be another one of the many interrogations that Chapman had to go through. Chapman was asked again why he hated England. Chapman told them the long drawn-out story. He was told that he would be trained in many areas of espionage. It would include operating a radio set, learning Morse code, parachuting, writing in secret Ink, how to fire a pistol. But most important of all and what really excited Chapman, he would be taught everything he needed to know about his favourite subject, explosives. Chapman was given a room at the top of the house. And told to learn to speak German all times. His room was small but it was lavishly decorated. It was comfortable though simple. Compared with the life he had been used to, this was sheer luxury.

Before long other officers turned up and would require more interrogations. Chapman had to repeat the story again and again. But as time passed Chapman trained and trained. One aspect of the training would be parachuting. He would be expected one day to be parachuted into England where he would commence his spying. On one occasion a parachute training jump went seriously wrong. Chapman landed face down on a concrete runway which knocked several of his front teeth out. The Germans arranged some expensive dental treatment which left Chapman with three gold teeth.

The longer he was at the villa the Germans began to trust Chapman and they began to like him, and Chapman liked them as well. Chapman slowly became friendly with his new captors and began to enjoy their hospitality. He was allowed to walk round the grounds, but he had to have a guard with him. Eventually he was allowed to walk the grounds without a guard provided he stuck to the rules and regulations and never ventured out of the confines of the villa grounds. Chapman became lonely so they allowed Chapman to have a pet. The pet was a pig that he could train to take for walks just like a dog. Chapman named the pig Bobby. This was probably a joke on the British police, [not exactly a term of endearment] who were always after him.

Eventually Chapman was allowed to go into the town as long as he had two armed guards with him and he spoke only German. He went to the clubs where there were German officers. The story was that Chapman was born in Germany but had lived in America for most of his life. He even got up to his tricks with women in the town and providing he had his guards with him there was no problem. Chapman became a friend of the Germans and the Germans became friends of Chapman. Dr Graumann was the officer in charge of Chapman and was keeping a close eye on him. In fact Dr Graumann wasn't his real name, it was actually Stephen von Greonning. Even with his friendship with the Germans Chapman wasn't stupid and while he was in the villa he would spy on the Germans. He never forgot how badly he was treated at Romainville prison and how the SS guards were quite happy to remove someone for execution for some petty revenge and that his good friend Anthony Faramus was still stuck in the Paris hellhole. He never wrote anything down, he purely committed everything to memory. Names, conversations, when and which people were visiting. He believed this could be very useful if he was ever caught in England. Chapman also suspected that von Greonning may not agree with everything Hitler was doing. He overheard conversations listening through keyholes.

One day when everyone was away he was in his room and he decided to search around the house looking in drawers making mental notes of what he found. On one occasion he ventured into the attic and to his amazement he found a cartoon drawn on the wall, someone had drawn Adolf Hitler as a carrot. It was most likely known that the picture was there but it just shows that maybe his captors were not all in favour of the Nazi regime but had to toe the line. One day Chapman decided to go to town by himself, though this was obviously against the rules. He was going into the bars and clubs. He was then recognised by member of the Gestapo, he was apprehended and taken back to the villa. There he was given a dressing down by von Greonning and told on no account with ever to leave the villa again on his own. Chapman was told that should he ever break the rules again he will be sent back to Romainville Prison, in future armed guards would be with him at all times.

More training, more waiting around, and Chapman starts to become bored. The Germans recognise this so they sent him to an explosives expert in Berlin. He was taught everything he needed to know about explosives, which chemicals to use, which compounds react with each other, to understand the amounts of ingredients to use to form the size of certain bombs. He was then returned to Villa Bretoniere. He was allowed to practice blowing things up in the garden. Chapman made himself bombs which he detonated. The Germans would be involved in meetings in the house when all of a sudden a loud blast rattled the windows. It was Chapman practising in the garden. One day von Groening asked Chapman to remove an old tree stump at the bottom of the garden. To give him some practice away from the confines of the villa. Chapman used far too much explosives. He set the detonator and luckily he ran for it. There was a massive explosion and a burning tree stump launched hundred metres into the air landed into the garden of a house across the street. Complaints were received and Chapman was stopped from his dangerous activities.

Chapman was told that his first mission will soon be arranged and in the meantime, the Germans gave him the code name Fritz though he was always known as Fritzen (*little Fritz*). He was told to improve his radio Morse code. Chapman was allowed to send test messages back and forth to the *Abwehr* communications office in Paris. He would tend to make small silly jokes which the Germans did not really understand. One of the messages he sent referred to his pet Bobby the pig. "YOUR FRIEND BOBBY THE PIG GORES LIKE A KING EATS LIKE A LION AND SHITS LIKES AN ELEPHANT" FRITZ. The German receiving station couldn't understand the joke and did not see the humour. Nevertheless they were not the only ones listening out. The Radio Security Service (RSS) in England was the wireless intercept organisation who were working on behalf the MI6. They were listening out for clandestine radio stations and intercepted that message. As the coded message was sent in groups of five letters it was a good probability that it originated from the *Abwehr*, who typically used that format. The message was immediately passed onto Bletchley Park. The codebreakers decrypted the message then in turn sent on to MI5 who were monitoring the possibility of spies being infiltrated into Britain. They are now aware that there was an agent called Fritz being trained and it's a good possibility that he will soon be parachuted into England. Agent Fritz gave away a little tell-tale sign of his transmissions to prove to the Germans it was him. He would always start the message, FFFFF and end the message with HI HU HA HA HA.

The mission

It was time for Chapman to be given his first mission before he got into any more mischief. It started with an interview with von Groening. Before his mission once again Chapman was interrogated to check that he really did hate the English. Once the Germans had confidence in Chapman they asked him what he actually did in England. He repeated once again that he broke into banks and blew open the safe with gelignite. The German said "well we have a job for you. We want you to blow up something for us". Chapman enquired what the job involved. von Groening replied "We want you to blow up the De Havilland aircraft factory in Hatfield (North of London). Chapman was quite surprised as this request was not the normal size of the job that he was used to. Nevertheless Chapman agreed to do the job. The Germans would raise a contract to state that he would receive 150,000 Reichsmarks for the success of the operation. Chapman thought it was about £15,000 hence this amount of money could set him up for life. In fact it was only £250 in those days, probably only about £10,000 now.

Chapman was told he would be parachuted into Britain

then he was to make contacts with his old criminal friends. The Germans would give him enough money to pay them, obtain explosives and blow up the power plant that supplied De Havilland with its electricity. Chapman was asked to sign a contract which clearly stated if he cheated on the Germans he would be summarily executed and furthermore told that if he failed to pay the tax due on the money they paid him he would face prosecution. The contract was probably worthless anyway because everyone was signing with their false names. Chapman had been allocated the codename Fritz, his Mission to be known as Operation Walter.

The mosquito aircraft.

The De Havilland aircraft factory in Hatfield was responsible for building the mosquito bomber, a very successful versatile aircraft. The aircraft was hated by the Germans especially Hermann Goering, who was the commander-in-chief of the Luftwaffe. Goering wanted the destruction of the factory to prevent any more these aircraft being manufactured. The mosquito aircraft was designed in early 1940 and built from wood. Its versatility was incredible with high altitude reconnaissance to low altitude accurate bombing raids. German night fighters were almost powerless to intercept it. The mosquito was used by the RAF into the 1950s when it was replaced by a jet powered aircraft. This small wooden aircraft known as the "wooden wonder" or by its pilots as the "mossie" was a pain in the side of the German air force so they wanted it destroyed along with its factory.

Chapman's training had been completed; he knew exactly what he had to do and was more than happy to get on with the job. But all this changed, on 11 November 1942 as German forces invaded the unoccupied zone of Southern France. Until now the French government was controlled by Marshall Philippe Petain from the town of Vichy which had now capitulated to the Nazis.

The *Abwehr* which was part of the German army now has to toe the military line. Chapman's mission has been put on hold. The mainly civilian-looking *Abwehr* officers, now have to wear uniforms and carry arms. Their organisation becomes known as the *Abwehrkommandos*. Chapman enjoyed wearing his new German army uniform. The first mission would be to attack some villages in what was Vichy France and to arrest any possible resistance personnel. This is probably the darker side of Chapman's life with the Germans. He enjoyed going into villages banging on doors arresting suspects in their houses, in their shops and in their workplaces. He would take them for interrogation. Chapman enjoyed this but he had second thoughts. He realised what would happen to these people that he arrested. He remembered what happened to him when he was arrested in Jersey and thrown into a Gestapo prison. So he decided to let all his suspects go free. The operation was eventually cancelled and he was sent back to Villa de la Bretoniere to continue with Operation Walter.

Operation Walter

All plans were agreed, Operation Walter was given the go-ahead.
Agent Fritz was to be taken to the airfield and flown across the
channel. They would then fly low to avoid radar. The drop site
was to be in Cambridgeshire. The plan was that Fritz would
make his way to London and get in contact with his past felons,
obtain explosives and blow up the De Havilland Power plant in
Hatfield. On the evening of 15th December 1942 Fritz arrived at
Le Bourget airfield, north-east of Paris, in his kit bag he had all
the equipment he required including a wireless set, colt revolver,
compass, maps, and an ID card of George Clarke of
Hammersmith and £990 in used bank notes. Fritz climbed
through the hatch of the Focke Wolf aircraft at 11 o'clock at
night. Twenty-five minutes later the aircraft was speeding down
the runway. Operation Walter had begun. Meanwhile MI5 had
been receiving messages from Bletchley Park regarding agent
Fritz who was to be dropped in Cambridgeshire in the early
hours of 16th December MI5 and Special Branch headed for the
proposed drop zone. Coastal Command were also alerted and
told to send up some anti-aircraft flack but not to shoot down the
lone enemy aircraft. As the Focke Wolf flew across the English
Channel, it was spotted and it was reported that an aircraft was
seen circling at low altitude. Fritz is ready to jump, as the green
jump light is illuminated by the exit, he stands by the door and
edges forward, but with his pack on his back and his parachute
he could not fit through the aircraft door. As the aircrew pushed
and shoved he just would not fit. The Focke Wolf has to go
around again. This time as Fritz stood at the door, and the green

light went on he felt the mighty kick of a jackboot in his back. Fritz was floating down to the Cambridgeshire soil rather faster than expected, owing to a damaged panel in his parachute. Fritz lost consciousness for a moment, but he awoke to a large thud as he landed face-down onto wet farm land. He finally came round covered in blood from a nosebleed and caked with mud from the ploughed field.

The first thing was to bury his parachute, and then find out where he had landed. He made his way across the field until he reached a road. He couldn't find his roadmap which the Germans gave to him, so he started to walk along a small country road in darkness. After a time he spots a house in the light of the quarter moon. He could see the house had a telephone wire from a pole. He makes his way along a small lane to the front door. This small farm cottage was the home of Martha and George Covine they were farmworkers. Martha was already awake as she had heard the sound of the aircraft circling overhead. She is now disturbed again with banging on her front door. As her husband George snored away in his bed dead to the world, Martha makes her way downstairs with a large rolling pin in her hand. She unbolts the front door to be confronted by a tall skinny man covered in mud with blood running down his face, in his high-pitched voice he says "I think I have had an accident." And then asks "Do you have a telephone? I must call the police."

Chapman explained to Mrs Covine that he was a British airman and that he had just arrived from France. He telephones the police and was put through to Littleport Police Station in Ely Cambridgeshire. PC Guy Hill arrives at 3.15am. The police station at Wisbech 19 miles away, had already been on alert since they heard the plane overhead earlier, they had also learned of a possible German agent being dropped by parachute. The police had been informed by MI5 that this situation was to be known as Operation Nightcap. This was MI5's plan to apprehend Agent Fritz. Eddie Chapman was an expert in telling stories, he had quite an imaginative mind and he was an excellent liar. So, until the Wisbech police arrived, Mrs Covine made mugs of tea and Chapman fed her and PC Guy Hill with all his tales, most of them fabricated. Eventually at 04:30 Sergeants Vale and Hutchings arrived. In the living room of the house, Chapman told the police that he had arrived from France. He showed them his kit, and handed over the pistol and the ammunition. He told the police that his name was George Clarke then told them that they must inform British Intelligence as he couldn't discuss anything further. They then all left for Wisbech police station to wait for MI5 officers to collect him. Meanwhile, after all the excitement, Martha Covine went back to bed, and her husband stirred. Martha told him of her exploits with George Clarke (Chapman / Fritz) and the police. Her husband said "Go back to sleep, woman, you must have been dreaming!" But Martha had been told by the officers not to murmur a word of this to anyone, and she kept the secret for many years.

Meanwhile, Chapman had been collected from Wisbech police station by MI5 officers and was taken to camp 020 in at Ham, close to Richmond Surrey. Camp 020 at Latchmere House was the interrogation centre for all captured spies, or even foreign spies who volunteered to work for Britain.

The Camp Commandant Lieutenant Colonel Robin "Tin Eye" Stephens, was never seen without his monocle hence his nickname. His officers even believed that he went to sleep at night with it in. So he became known as "old Tin Eye". Stephens was a very strict commandant as would be expected. He never used torture to extract information from a suspect, his severe non-violent interrogations and questioning would normally do the trick. Eddie Chapman once again in his life found himself locked in a prison cell. As he sat there, he reflected on his time with the Germans in France, the hard times he had in Romainville Prison, and wondered if the Germans looked after his friend Anthony Faramus who he had to leave behind, and even if he was still alive.

Eventually, the cell door unlocked, and Chapman was taken in for interrogation. Once in the interview room, Chapman told his new captors that his name is Edward Chapman, and not George Clarke, as was on his identity card. He gave his interrogators the full story from beginning to end, including the plan for Operation Walter, the proposed blowing-up of the De Havilland factory. He also told them everything that he found out about his German captors when he spied on them at Villa Bretoniere. Day after day, he had to repeat his story. His interrogators made notes to make sure it was the same each time, and it was. Camp 020 tied up his story with the decrypts from Bletchley Park including the Bobby the Pig transmissions. Then an interview was arranged with Thomas Argyle Robertson, known as TAR as per his initials, the head of MI5 B1a the double-cross section.

Eddie Chapman fell into this category. When interviewed it was established that he would be happy to return to France as a double agent But first he had to show the Germans that he could be trusted to do what he had been sent to England for, to blow up the De Havilland aircraft factory at Hatfield. Chapman was sent back to his cell and waited. He was sad that the enemy treated him so well, wining and dining him, and how his own country treated him like a criminal, but then he probably thought "I suppose I am a criminal".

He told his captors that if he did not send a radio message soon to France, the Germans would believe that he had been caught and possibly being controlled by the British. All spies working as double cross agents, were never allowed to work alone. They would be allocated detectives to keep an eye on them and a case officer to work with them and sometimes operate a radio. The case officer would learn to mimic the style known as the "fist" of the Morse operator, so that if the spy could not or would not send a message the case officer could take over their radio transmitter. MI5 B1a allocated Chapman with a case officer who was an ex BBC radio engineer, Captain Ronnie Reed. Reed set up a temporary aerial in the grounds of Camp 020. So Chapman could send his first signal back to the Germans. There was a time lapse while Chapman was being interrogated, so Fritz sent his first signal back, telling the Germans that the delay was due to his having to get his radio repaired as it got damaged during the parachute drop. He started his message with FFFFF and ended with HI HU HA HA HA. The message would have been encrypted into the Abwehr hand cipher, and monitored the by the Radio Security Service to ensure that he was sending exactly what he was told to send no more and no less.

After more meetings and interrogations, Chapman left Camp 020 and was taken to an MI5 safe house at 35 Crespigny Road, Hendon in North London. The next job for Chapman was to blow up de Havilland, but Chapman was not allowed to go off on his own. He was allocated two Special Branch Officers who would be with him at all times. Corporal Paul Blackwell and Lance Corporal Allen Tooth would be with Chapman everywhere he went. Chapman and his merry men went to Hatfield, North of London to do a recognisance of the De Havilland aircraft factory. Chapman drew maps and made notes. No one seemed to notice him. The plans were to blow up the power plant which would stop production of the Mosquito aircraft. The notes went back to MI5 B1a who realised that if the factory power plant was to be blown up, the Germans would arrange a photographic reconnaissance trip. Therefore it had to look like it had been really been blown up. It was arranged that the set designers from the Old Vic Theatre in London would be used to design a facade to go over the roof of the De Havilland power plant which would make it look from the air as if it was badly damaged and out of action. Tarpaulins were painted and placed on the roof of the power plant. Broken brick walls were made out of wood also replica plastic power transformers were to be laid on their side to give the impression of an explosion. Then explosives had to be arranged to set off a big bang which had to be heard at a far distance to make it all as realistic as possible. Firstly, the RAF had to confirm that the camouflage looked authentic from the air. Colonel Sir John Turner head of air ministry camouflage section and TAR Robertson arranged for an RAF aircraft to photograph and make sure that the De Havilland power plant looked well and truly out of action.

Chapman sent a message to his German contacts that he was ready to perform Operation Walter. On the night of the 29th/30th January, Hatfield in Hertfordshire, was rocked by a massive explosion. On Monday 1st February 1943, The Daily Express reported that there was an explosion at a factory in the outskirts of London and that investigations were being made. Chapman reported back that his mission had been accomplished. Von Groening was over the moon with delight and told Chapman not to hurry back to France, but MI5 needed Chapman in France as soon as possible. But how does Agent Fritz get back to France? The RAF couldn't just drop him back in. In the meantime, our amateur explosives expert was to meet Britain's leading explosives expert. Lord Victor Rothschild was working for MI5, MI6 and SOE (Special Operations Executive). He was involved with anti-sabotage, and what the Germans were up to in the field of bomb-making. Who better than Eddie Chapman who had been trained in that field by a top German scientist in Berlin? Many hours were spent together, the London crook and the Peer of the Realm. These two men were at each end of the social scale but they had so much in common they would have loved to work with each other. They had one mutual interest: blowing things up.

It was time for Fritz to return to his German friends, but

first, Chapman had to have a really good alibi. MI5 B1a, along with Ronnie Reed, created a story from the moment Fritz hit the Cambridgeshire mud to when he would meet up again with the Germans. He had to say exactly who he met, where he had been living and what he had been doing every hour of the day since he arrived in England. MI5 knew that he would be interrogated again and again. The Germans would try and trip him up, so a practice place was set up at Camp 020 where they imitated a German interrogation scenario. He was tested and retested, trapped into giving the incorrect answers, but 020 could not trip Chapman up. He was good; he had to be otherwise it would cost him his life. Chapman told MI5 that he wanted to do something that people would remember him by. He said that he had told von Groening that he would like to go to one of Hitler's rallies. He said that if he could get a place in the audience close enough to where Hitler was speaking, he would shoot him. Chapman knew it would mean certain death for him, but he reckoned that he'd had a good life. But MI5 B1a knew that he would not be allowed anywhere near Hitler and that Hitler had extremely good security, also that this kind of action would endanger all of Britain's agents working the double-cross system.

MI5 were now happy that Chapman had his alibi story perfect, and it was time for him to be sent back to France. It was decided that Chapman would travel via Lisbon. Portugal was neutral during World War II. There were semi-regular flights, but many ships would also travel the dangerous route across U-boat infested waters. MI5 arranged a fake identity: He would become Hugh Anson, the name taken from one of his past villain colleagues that was safely locked away in prison in at the time in the North of England. Forged papers and ID cards were produced. The *City of Lancaster* was a 3000 ton merchant ship that Chapman was to board and work as a steward. Captain Reginald Kearon was informed by MI5 that Hugh Anson would be working on-board, but when it arrived in Lisbon he would probably jump ship. The captain was handed a large parcel that had to be locked in the ship's safe. He was made fully aware of Chapman's mission and was handed a parcel which contained Chapman's gun, money and newspaper cuttings of the De Havilland explosion. All this was to be given to Chapman when the ship arrived in Lisbon. Captain Kearon was sworn to secrecy and told that he must not mention a word to anybody.

Chapman eventually joined the ship as the Captain's steward. The voyage was not without some issues as Chapman picked fights with some of the crew. Eventually, they reached Lisbon, and Chapman alighted. The hunt now began for the *Abwehr* offices, but this was not without difficulty. Chapman had to visit the German embassy, secret meetings were arranged at coffee bars with undercover agents. Eventually he was able to make contact. The original plan was that the Germans would arrange to send him back to France. But once he made contact, he was treated with suspicion. The Germans had to be sure that their agent Fritz was now not working for the British, so the interrogation commenced. He had to put into practice his Camp 020 training, as he had to repeat his story over again and again. Without one single error. Chapman was not happy about the ways that the Germans were treating him. He told the Germans "if you don't trust me, I will prove to you that I am loyal, I will blow up my own ship." the *City of Lancaster*, which is moored up in the port.

The Germans took him at his word. They said "we will pay you if you plant a bomb on your ship". They soon supplied Chapman with a coal bomb, basically a large lump of Coal that had been hollowed out and packed with high explosives. Chapman agreed to take the bomb back on-board the *City of Lancaster* and place it deep into ship's coal bunker, when the ships stoker would unknowingly shovel the bomb into the furnace it would explode, taking the ship to the bottom of the Atlantic. Chapman collected the special bomb and took it on-board the *City of Lancaster*. But as Chapman arrived and boarded his ship instead of placing it in the coal bunker, he walked into Captain Kearan's office, put his hand down his trousers and produced what looked like a lump large of coal and placed it on the Captain's table. Chapman explained to the captain that it was a bomb and to take great care with it. When you get back to England, make sure this is passed on to British Intelligence. After this event, the Germans again had trust in Agent Fritz, even though he never did blow up his ship, the *City of Lancaster*. After more interrogations, Chapman was told that the Nantes office had closed down and he was to be sent to Norway. Chapman asked about the money that the Germans were supposed to pay him for the De Havilland job. He was told that he would be paid in Norway. But first Chapman was sent to Paris by train and from there on to Berlin for yet more interrogations before he was flown to Oslo.

As Chapman makes his way through the terminal building of Oslo airport, there waiting for him was Dr Graumann alias Stefan von Groening. They embraced like old friends. Von Groening told Fritz that the German's required another interrogation. Board and lodging were arranged and the following day the interrogations began. He had again to tell his story that M15 had fabricated for him. The German's would be checking every word for any discrepancies. Chapman asked about his money, von Groening said "before we talk about money look at this" he placed a small box of the table in front of Fritz, "You are the only British Citizen that has ever been awarded the Iron Cross," von Groening continued. "It has been awarded for your bravery by the Fuhrer for destroying the De Havilland factory and blowing up your ship." Chapman was astonished that he had received such an award, as it so happened he did neither, it then passed through his mind what would happen to him should the Germans find out that none of it was true. von Groening gave him some money on account. Chapman was not happy but he had no choice as he was not in a position to argue with the Germans. He was then let loose within reason. He frequented bars and clubs where the German's congregated. He made friends with German officers and met Norwegian women.

One evening at a German officer's club, at the Ritz bar in Skillebekk, in the west of Oslo Chapman met a stunning brunette Norwegian woman, Dagmar Lahlum. They became attracted to each other like magnets. Eventually, Dagmar moved in with Chapman at the safe house that the Germans provided at

Kapelveien 15, Oslo. Chapman needed more money, von Groening gave him some more on account. Chapman had always wanted a sailboat now he craved to take Dagmar sailing on the beautiful fjords surrounding Oslo. The Germans agreed and bought him a small yacht, which he learned to sail, and took Dagmar out with him. They would sail for hours around the little islands in Oslo-fjord, they were truly in love. One day they were having a romantic meal together when Dagmar took the chance of her life. In fact, had she got it wrong it would have clearly cost her, her life. She admitted to Chapman that she was working for the Norwegian resistance. What followed broke all the rules of MI5, if he had got it wrong, and if Dagmar was lying, this would certainly have cost him his life. He admitted to Dagmar that he was working for the British Intelligence.

To avoid Chapman getting bored before his next assignment for the Germans, he was required to brush up on his Morse code radio sending. As he improved, the Germans asked Chapman to train two Icelandic spies in radio procedure, Bjornsson and Juliusson, who would when trained be sent to Iceland to spy on British ships in Icelandic ports

Meanwhile in London, MI5 were becoming very concerned about the whereabouts of their agent Zigzag. MI5 has had no contact with Chapman for months. They were starting to wonder if he had been caught, and if so, would he talk and possibly blow the double-cross system. Or is it possible that he has switched sides and is now working for the Germans? In reality, Chapman was having the time of his life. With Dagmar by his side, a luxury apartment paid for by the Third Reich, wining, dining, sailing... Oh, what a lovely war! But the Germans believed Fritz would still be faithful to them for future operations while they continued to owe him money, which was only paid out to him in small doses.

June 1944, Fritz was summoned to von Groening's office where he is told that there is another important mission for him. With the Allied successes of operation overlord Fritz is sent to Berlin where he was to be given details of his next job. Chapman packed his bags, said farewell to von Groening as an old friend. Von Groening and Fritz came to an arrangement that after the war they would go into partnership together and purchase a small bar in Paris. Fritz thought he was to be paid the outstanding balance of the cash the Germans owed him, but it was not to be, that would come later. Then there was Dagmar. A difficult situation as these two lovers were to be torn apart. Chapman told Dagmar that he would return so they could marry one day. For Dagmar, difficult times lay ahead as she became ostracised, since all her friends believed she was living with and entertaining a German spy. Of course, she could never reveal that Chapman was on their side.

Fritz arrived in Berlin, and was interrogated yet again. The Germans again thoroughly checked every detail. They were now using revenge weapons against Britain. The V1 - more commonly known as the "flying bomb", or "doodlebug" – was an unpiloted craft which was aimed with a launcher at Britain, kept on course by a giro, and when its fuel was exhausted (due to a timer cut-out switch), it plummeted to the ground causing a massive explosion. The Germans were aiming them at Central

London, but due to reporting restrictions in the British Press, they were unsure whether they were on target. There was also a new weapon, the V2, which was probably the world's first long-range ballistic missile. It was a rocket loaded with high explosives, 1000 kilograms of Amatol which was a lethal amount of TNT mixed with ammonium nitrate. It was launched from mobile launchers. The rocket would rise into the upper atmosphere and then descend on its target like a bolt out of the blue. With no warning, a V2 rocket could destroy a whole street in one attack, V standing for "*Vergeltungswaffe*" – "Retribution weapon". The Germans wanted Fritz to go to Britain and report back on the accuracy of these weapons. Were they hitting their target? The Germans also required knowledge of public opinion. "Was there a feeling of hopelessness and was the population ready to surrender?"

Once again plans were being made to parachute agent Fritz back to England. Meanwhile, in England, MI5 B1a were about to write off Agent Zigzag as for many months no one had heard anything from him. They believed he was possibly dead. MI5 were just about to close down his files, when something really interesting occurred. In Iceland, two spies had been caught, they were arrested, and sent to Britain for interrogation. They arrived at Camp 020 and interrogated by Lieutenant Colonel Robin Stephens. The two spies, Bjornsson and Juliusson both told the same story that they were trained in Norway to operate their radios by a thin man who seemed to have an English accent, with a high-pitched voice and a moustache. Stephens started to realise that this could possibly be Eddie

Chapman. After further questioning it was obvious that Chapman was still alive and operating, but was he now working for the Germans?

The Germans sent Fritz back to Britain, and again he was parachuted into Cambridgeshire, once back he contacted MI5, who immediately interrogated him. MI5 wanted to know every move he had made while he had been away. Chapman told them everything he found out about the German network in Norway: People, places, and names. The Germans had given their trusted agent Fritz a Leica camera as a gift. Chapman had taken photographs of German officers and buildings at great risk to himself and brought them back to England hidden on his person. Also, Chapman told them that he was sent back to report on the accuracy of the V weapons. Though they were landing on target the Germans were oblivious of this, so Chapman was sent to England for this reason. We knew that the Germans were completely unaware of their accuracy, so it was arranged for reports to be sent back to the Germans that would confirm to them that their V weapons were landing too far North West of London. Therefore they needed to change their aim further to the South East. The Germans believed this since they were also receiving similar reports from another one of their spy's agent Arabel. Of course, Arabel was also working for MI5, as a double agent and known as Garbo. With this information, the aim was altered and central London was avoided. This unfortunately had the effect of V bombs landing in South East London, and in parts of Kent, the idea being that these areas would have been far less populated.

D Day had passed and Allied troops were well on their way battling through France towards Germany. The Battle of the Atlantic was turning in our favour, being helped by Bletchley Park's Ultra Intelligence, which was used to attack German U Boats. The RAF was also assisted by the new long range American aircraft, the Liberator. MI5 put Chapman up in a safe house in Mayfair, a very smart part of London. Chapman broke all the rules again, arranging wild parties and entertained his old criminal friends. Meanwhile, his faithful case officer and friend Ronnie Reed was needed elsewhere, and a new case officer was allocated to Chapman. Eddie Chapman and Ronnie Reed were not only colleagues but also good friends, they were very sorry to part. At their final meeting Eddie Chapman gave Ronnie Reed something to remember him by and that was the Iron Cross that Stefan von Groening gave to him in Norway. As a matter of fact Ronnie Reid's son still has that Iron Cross today.

Michael Ryde had joined MI5 through his father-in-law who also worked for the service, prior to that Ryde was a chartered accountant who liked his drink and could become very disagreeable in the wrong company and to him Chapman was the wrong company. Ryde did not like Chapman, and he did not trust him. He knew Chapman was taking liberties with the service, and he was determined to catch him out. But there was one more job for Chapman to do first.

In the Battle of the Atlantic, the Allies now had the upper hand, U boats sailing on the surface made for easy spoils. The Allies could not let the Germans know that Ultra Intelligence was giving away the U boats positions, and so the Allies invented a weapon that didn't really exist, and then made the Germans think that it did. This was a job for Agent Zigzag. The weapon was called Squid. Squid was a real weapon that actually existed on destroyers but it was to be notionally enhanced to make the Germans believe it was a new secret weapon. The idea was that it could be launched from a ship, home-in on a submerged U boat, chase it for several thousand metres, and then make contact and detonate. Of course, there was no such weapon, but information about this secret weapon filtered through to the Germans via our double-cross agents. The Cossor radio manufacturer in England which was now making armaments was to produce a set of blueprints for this non-existent weapon. If the Germans believed this, the hope was that they would think that this was the reason that so many of their U Boats were being lost. The Germans fell for this deception. Their reaction was for all U boats to sail on the surface where possible, which made them easy pickings for the Allied air forces to sink them.

Chapman was now living it up in his Mayfair apartment provided by MI5. One night, Chapman organised a party, more what you would call nowadays, a rave. Plenty of booze, lots of girls and some of his former criminal fraternity. Michael Ryde, Chapman's new case officer, waiting to pounce with a colleague, approached Chapman's flat and knocked on the door. The party was in full swing, loud music, booze, etc. The MI5 men were invited in by Chapman. A rather drunken Soho villain friend of Chapman's Billy Hill saw these two rather official-looking men, and called out to them "Are you sending Eddie away on one of his secret missions?" Ryde now had all the ammunition that he needed. Eddie Chapman was fired. A breach of trust and now a loose cannon. Chapman never worked for MI5 again. His operation was taken over by another agent, posing as Agent Fritz. As far as Eddie Chapman was concerned, he was paid off and for his work as Agent Zigzag, and had all his past misdemeanours written off. He was now a free man.

After the war as you would have expected Eddie Chapman did not allow himself to become bored. All his life he needed excitement. Chapman hired two private detectives to look for Betty Farmer. Then one day completely by chance Eddie found Betty in a London Hotel where he just happened to be having a meal. The last time Betty saw Eddie was when he'd jumped through the window of the Hotel de La Plage Jersey in Jersey before the war. They eventually married. Betty Farmer had one daughter. Eddie Chapman became quite a wealthy man after the MI5 payoff, along with the money that the Germans gave him, which he was allowed to keep. He then purchased a small old cargo ship, The *Earl Grey*. It started as a legitimate business taking various cargos around Britain and Ireland. He eventually sold his ship and bought an aircraft so he could take goods usually, contraband to places people normally couldn't get to. But Eddie Chapman soon returned to the world of villainy, extortion, blackmail, fixing dog races. He was also became involved in dodgy property deals involving well known international construction companies on the Gold Coast of Africa. Though he found himself in court on many occasions he never went back to prison. It is the conjecture that the authorities seem to always turn a blind eye to Eddie Chapman's activities.

He purchased Shenley Lodge in Hertfordshire and turned it into a health spa, bought a Rolls-Royce and a castle in Ireland. Chapman even located and invited his old German friend and colleague Stefan von Groening to the wedding of his daughter. He never let on about his wartime secrets to his German friend. Eventually he bought a house in the Canary Islands. Eddie Chapman was disappointed that back in the 1950s the British Government banned the News of the World newspaper from publishing his memoirs, "the Eddie Chapman story", though they were published in France and Chapman was fined £50 for breaking the Official Secrets Act. There was a BBC TV documentary called "Underworld" transmitted on 16 February 1994, narrated by Bob Hoskins, which was released in Chapman's final years.

On 11 December 1997 Chapman died at the age of 83 of heart failure. In Oslo Dagmar Larlem, Chapman's war time lover had never married and she kept the secret to her detriment as she was imprisoned for six months for apparently fraternising with the German agent. They met up only once after the war in Chapman's later life.

Anthony Faramus, Chapman's friend from Jersey whom he left in the Romainville prison in Paris, was sent to several concentration camps where he was starved and almost died. He miraculously survived the war with broken ribs and malnutrition. He wrote his autobiography and appeared in films. One of these films was called the "Triple Cross" a 1966 Anglo-

French co-produced film directed by Terence Young and produced by Jacques-Paul Bertrand about the Eddie Chapman story. However he did write one book about his post war escapades called Free Agent Being the Further Adventures of Eddie Chapman published by Alan Wingate London 1955.

As far as the Eddie Chapman story is concerned, the Germans were never completely sure whether Chapman was working for them or the British. Likewise British Intelligence were never quite sure whether Chapman was working for them or for the Germans. To be perfectly honest I am not sure whether Chapman knew himself. But through his bravery Eddie Chapman helped save thousands of lives by diverting V1 and V2 rockets from central London, and saving a vital aircraft factory in Hertfordshire from destruction. He also created diversions for U-boats by convincing the Germans of a secret anti-submarine weapon that never existed. But all this was mixed in with his love for women, usually several relationships at the same time. And not forgetting his love for money, loads of it. But most of all Eddie Chapman was the spy who loved himself.

John Cairncross (The Fifth Man)

I find it absolutely incredible that with all the extreme secrecy surrounding Bletchley Park during World War II that a spy working for the Soviets could remove hundreds of secret documents in just four years without anyone noticing.

There have been stories about John Cairncross from several eminent historians. Even John Cairncross wrote his own autobiography "The Enigma spy". But the problem is what or who should you believe, the archives that have been released by our security services, ex-Soviet spies of the KGB, or John Cairncross himself? I will leave you to make up your own mind.

Soviet intelligence organisations:

NKVD 1934 – 1946. (Sometimes referred to as KGB)

The People's Commissariat for Internal Affairs.

NKGB 1943 – 1946. (Sometimes referred to as KGB)

People's Commissariat for State Security

MGB   1946 – 1954   (Sometimes referred to as KGB)

Ministry for State Security.

KGB   1954 -1991.

Committee for State Security.

Born in Lesmahago in Lanarkshire, Cairncross was one of four brothers and three sisters. His father was an ironmonger and his mother was a schoolteacher. All his brothers became professors. He attended Glasgow University where he won an open scholarship to study French and German. Next he studied at the Sorbonne University in Paris, he also travelled around France and Germany and made friends. It was while touring Germany that he could see for himself that the rise of the Nazis was going to be a problem for Europe. In 1934 then aged 21 after Glasgow and Sorbonne he won a scholarship to Trinity College Cambridge. It was there he studied modern languages. Though coming from a humble background, he possessed a brilliant intellect. In 1935 he started to attend political gatherings. Though he attended communist meetings he claimed never to have been a member of the Communist Party. Anthony Blunt, a college colleague who had a room above that of Cairncross, noted that he could be at times unsociable, cantankerous and arrogant. Nevertheless Blunt, a talent spotter for the NKVD, thought that Cairncross could be a possible future agent.

As Cairncross prepared to leave Cambridge after successful marks in his Tripos (final examinations) he claimed that he was never approached or offered a job in academia, which would normally have been expected with such a brilliant intellect and results. So it was suggested that he found a position in the Foreign Office.

After attaining top marks in the civil service entrance exams he was appointed to the Foreign Office on 14 October 1936. At this juncture he was already a mole for the Soviets. Arnold Deutsche was head of the recruitment section of the NKVD. His network had already recruited Kim Philby, Guy Burgess, Donald Maclean and Anthony Blunt. James Klugman, also with the NKVD, was asked by his friend Deutsche to approach Cairncross as he knew him from his Trinity days.

His recruiter, James Klugman, was one of Cambridge's most influential Marxists. The approach was classic. Cairncross was invited to help Comintern, the international Communist movement, against Fascism. Cairncross was recruited as a Soviet spy and given the codename of LISZT. Cairncross possessed a hatred of the British establishment. He later recalled how Klugman insisted that if he wished to mingle with the higher echelons of society the Glaswegian accent would have to go. In 1938 and 1939 agent LISZT passed foreign office papers to the Russians for the first time. He was also passing on to the Russians details and names of senior politicians who wished to do a deal with Hitler.

In 1941 Cairncross had been promoted to the Cabinet office and became Private Secretary to Lord Hankey, Chancellor to the Duchy of Lancaster, a similar position to a minister without portfolio. At this time Lord Hankey was chairing the government's scientific advisory committee which was discussing the possibility of an atomic super weapon. Though Cairncross denied this, it is certainly a strong possibility that he could have passed this information onto the Soviets. This had

Spies Lies and Double-cross Agents

been highly suspected due to released Russian information but unproven.

In 1942 Cairncross was called up to the Royal armoured Corps. As he was fluent in German and French and also the fact that he was working for Lord Hankey, this gave the Foreign Office a reasonable guarantee of his reliability. It is therefore understandable that without vetting he was transferred to the Government Code and Cypher School at Bletchley Park in Buckinghamshire. This was the British government's top secret code breaking establishment, where Cairncross was engaged at Hut 3, a department that dealt with the translation and analysis of decrypted enemy signals of the German air force and army.

Cairncross tells that life at Bletchley Park was very hard. There were eight hours of non-stop work with no recreation time. He would be taken back to his billet in one of the local villages within the area, then the following morning returning to complete another eight-hour shift. This is contrary to the stories of many of people who worked at Bletchley Park during the war, who say that there was time for recreation, with music societies, theatrical groups. Hut 12 was dedicated as a relaxation hut and Hut two, the NAAFI and library known as the beer hut. Interviews with veterans of Bletchley Park tell us of sports activities in the summer such as tennis and rounders, even rowing on the small lake. Maybe John Cairncross just did not want to mix in.

Meanwhile Cairncross's job at Hut 3 was the translation of messages of the German air force *Luftwaffe*. The name of these decrypts was 'Red' (Bletchley Park used coloured pencils to identify signals from different parts of the German military *Luftwaffe* was red). The messages were transcribed into readable texts to be passed on to the British military. The overall name of all deciphered messages was known as 'Ultra'. This was disseminated traffic from the German Enigma cipher machine and others cipher systems that the enemy was using, which were being intercepted and broken at Bletchley Park. Cairncross was astonished that the British did not trust the Soviets with ultra-intelligence. He now began passing information to his Soviet controller Anthony Gorski, which was immediately passed on to the NKVD then forwarded to Moscow for Stalin. Churchill had agreed to send only limited information to Stalin. (When it suited) Stalin, was not happy to receive intelligence from the west which he felt was untrustworthy. Also Stalin believed it was a small amount of the much bigger picture. Since it originated from Winston Churchill via Bletchley Park, it probably was. The danger was that the release of too much information could lead the Germans to find out that their Enigma system had been compromised. This would result in a quick change of enemy security procedures.

The Luftwaffe traffic that Hut 3 was analysing were mainly Enigma messages that were broken by Hut 6. Some of this concerned the German air force order of battle of Hitler's Operation *Unternehmen Zitadelle*. The Battle of Kursk was a Second World War engagement between German and Soviet forces on the Eastern Front near Kursk (450 kilometres or 280 miles south-west of Moscow) during July and August 1943.

Initially, the Soviets undertook a series of pre-emptive air strikes and simultaneously used Cairncross's information to develop a new anti-tank shell to penetrate the new thick German tank armour. The German offensive led to one of the largest armoured clashes in history, the Battle of *Prokhorovka*. The German offensive was met by two Soviet counter-offensives, Operation *Polkovodets Rumyantsev* and Operation *Kutuzov*. For the Germans the battle was the final strategic offensive that they were able to launch on the Eastern Front. Their extensive loss of men and tanks ensured that the victorious Soviet Red Army enjoyed the strategic initiative for the remainder of the war. In recognition of his critical assistance, Cairncross was awarded the Order of the Red Banner.

It is believed that Cairncross supplied the Soviets with over 5832 documents between 1941 and 1945. At the same time Kim Philby, Donald Maclean, Guy Burgess of MI6 and Anthony Blunt of MI5 were also supplying intelligence to Moscow. Stalin believed there was too much information supplied to Moscow and started to suspect that the amount of information supplied by the NKVD via their British spies was a multi-layered deception from the West (there's no pleasing some people). But the information supplied by Cairncross made an incredible difference to the Battle of the River Kursk, allowing the Russians to achieve massive pre-emptive strikes against German airfields, destroying over 500 enemy aircraft.

Yuri Modin was born in Russia on 8th November, 1922. Modin joined the KGB and in 1947 he was sent to London and became the main contact with what is now known as the

Cambridge ring of five. Modin felt that his position was becoming increasingly endangered through an intensification of the Security Service's inquiries about him.

At the end of the war, Cairncross was posted to the Treasury. Although he would later claim that he ceased working for the KGB after 1945, Yuri Modin tells a different story. Modin arrived in London in 1947 to meet up with Cairncross, Burgess and Blunt under the cover of a press attaché. According to Modin, "Everything flowed through the Treasury and Cairncross's information was perfect." Cairncross, whose Soviet code name was now Carelian. As Modin wrote in his memoirs in 1994, shown to Cairncross for approval prior to publication, "was my favourite of the Five". Modin's only complaint was that Cairncross was "a difficult man who was impolite to the aristocrats in the Civil Service. (We might ask who was responsible for giving John Cairncross a job in the Civil Service in the first place.)

In 1951 Scotland Yard raided the home of Guy Burgess. As they searched his flat they found several documents in handwriting that was not Burgess's. These documents were sent on to MI5, then just by chance one of the secretaries Evelyn Barnet recognised the style of writing. She stated that the writing was almost certainly that of a young civil servant by the name of John Cairncross of whom she knew worked at the Foreign Office before the war. In the early 1950s Cairncross became the Rome correspondent of the Economist magazine, he also worked for the Observer and the Canadian Broadcasting Corporation. From

1953 to 1960 Caincross worked for the United Nations in Geneva, and had other posts in the Far East and Pakistan.

An MI5 officer travelled to Rome to interview Cairncross. As this was outside the jurisdiction of the Official Secrets Act he made a complete confession of his treachery and his links with the KGB. James Klugman, codename OTTO, who was controlling Burgess, McLean and Philby, back in 1936 advised Cairncross to get himself into the Foreign Office which he did when the war was declared. He was sent to Bletchley Park which was controlled by MI6 who in turn were under the umbrella of the Foreign Office.

Peter Wright, the author of 'Spycatcher', travelled to Paris to meet Cairncross. Since Cairncross wanted to return to Britain. In his interview Cairncross told Wright that he had been working for British intelligence and that he had been passing information onto the Russians. But Cairncross claimed he was never a traitor, and that he only spied during the war when Russia was our ally. Even though he was a communist he only wanted to help the Russians during the war when they were on our side.

Cairncross claimed that while working at Bletchley Park he would find decrypts lying around and when no one was looking he would stuff them down his trousers. As he went home he walked past the armed guards on the gate, they never noticed a thing. These were then passed on to his agent OTTO who then forwarded them on to the NKVD. Cairncross was never prosecuted by the British authorities.

Even with his association with the other four, Philby, Burgess, Maclean and Blunt, Cairncross claims their motivation was completely different. Cairncross had been in Germany before the war and saw with his own eyes the actions of the Nazi thugs and the regime that was rising to power and he wanted to deal with this in his own way. As far as the other four were concerned he did not like them, in fact he detested them and what they stood for. Cairncross says he never got on with them, he felt that their ideology was some sort of prestigious folly.

John Cairncross wrote a book of his escapades called The Enigma Spy, An Autobiography: Century books London. – Subtitled "The Story of the Man Who helped Change the course of World War". He died 8th October 1995, aged 82 in Hertfordshire England.

Anthony Blunt

Blunt was a distant cousin of the late Queen Mother. Sir Anthony Blunt, KCVO, from 1956 to 1979 was a leading British art historian and adviser of art to Her Majesty the Queen. Blunt, who in 1964 after being offered immunity from prosecution, confessed to having been a Soviet spy. Queen Elizabeth II stripped Blunt of his knighthood, and he was removed as an Honorary Fellow of Trinity College. After his BBC Television confession at the age of 72, he broke down in tears.

He died: 26 March 1983, Westminster.

Guy Burgess

Burgess was a British radio producer, intelligence officer and Foreign Office official. He was a member of the Cambridge Five spy ring that passed Western secrets to the Soviets before and during the Cold War. He died: 30 August 1963, Moscow.

Donald Maclean

A British diplomat and member of the Cambridge Five who were spies for the Soviet Union. As an undergraduate, Maclean openly proclaimed his left-wing views, and was recruited into the Russian intelligence service. He died: 6 March 1983, Moscow, Russia

Kim Philby

A High-ranking member of British intelligence who worked as a double agent before defecting to the Soviet Union in 1963. He served as both an NKVD and KGB operative. Philby came very close to becoming the chief of MI6, "C" the Secret Intelligence Service. When he got to Moscow he found life wasn't as expected. He was no hero. He was treated as a ordiary citizen and he was never decorated for his work for the Soviets. He died: 11 May 1988, Moscow.

James Klugman

Generally known as James, codename OTTO, was a leading British Communist writer who became the official historian of the Communist Party of Great Britain. He died: 1977, Stockwell, London.

Arnold Deutsch

Sometimes described as Austrian, Czech or Hungarian, was an academic who worked as a Soviet spy, best known for having recruited Kim Philby. Much of his life remains unknown or disputed. He died: 7 November 1942.

Yuri Modin

Was born in Russia and was the Soviet controller of the Cambridge ring of five from 1948 to 1951. He published a book in France in 1994, the British abridged version was called 'My Five Cambridge Friends'. French original title, Mes Camarades de Cambridge, published in France in 1994.

The French version claimed that Victor Rothschild who was working for MI5 was the fifth man. The abridged version published in Britain was amended by historians who claimed it was John Cairncross. Yuri Modin died in 2007, Moscow.

Spies Lies and Double-cross Agents

Early homes of The Secret Intelligence Service MI6

Ashley Mansions Vauxhall Bridge Road.
In 1910 MI6 had a bogus address at the Post Office –
Messrs Rasen, Falcon Limited.

54 Broadway Buildings the home
of MI6 and GC&CS from 1922
Authors collection

No.2 Whitehall Court
Author's Collection

Eddie Chapman (Agent ZigZag)
National Archives

Dagmar Lahlum

Lilly Sergeueiew & Emil Kliemann
National Archives

Ewen Montagu & Team
Naval Intelligence Dept.
17M Room 13 at the Admiralty
Kind Permission Fiona Mason

Spies Lies and Double-cross Agents

Charles Cholmondeley & Ewen Montagu
en-route to Greenock with Major Martin on-board
Kind permission Jeremy Montagu

Admiral Wilhelm Canaris
Chief of the Abwehr
Bundesarchiv Bild 146-1979-013-43

Ewen Montagu
Kind Permission Fiona Mason

SIS Headquarters (MI6) Vauxhall Cross (VX) London

Author's Collection

MI5 Headquarters Millbank London

Author's Collection

British Type X Machine
Hut 3
Bletchley Park Trust

Enigma training
Bundesarchiv Bild 146-2005-0152
Photo o.Ang. I 1939/1945 ca.

Stephan von Gröning
Agent ZigZag's German Case Officer
Kind permission Maximilian von Groening

Lieutenant Colonel Robin "Tin Eye" Stephens
Imperial War Museum

Dusko Popov
National Archives

Commander A G Denniston's office at
Bletchley Park
Author's collection

Abwehr spy radio transmitter.
Authors' collection

M4 Enigma used by the U-Boats after
1st February 1942 on Triton Code (Shark)

Bletchley Park Trust

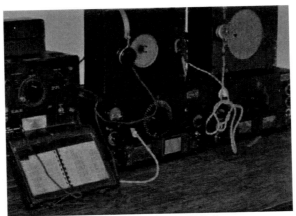

HRO Receiving equipment at Y Stations
Bletchley Park Trust

Eddie Chapman's protest of the UK Government's ban of his
"The Eddie Chapman Story"   in News of The World Newspaper
Associated Press

Spies Lies and Double Cross Agents

When you think of a spy what is conjured up in your mind? Possibly two men in trilby hats, whispering secrets to each in a dark corner or alleyway, or maybe you think of Ian Fleming's allegedly covert agent 007? I always find it strange that we call our secret agents, agents. Foreign agents we call spies. Spies have to remain invisible, no one should be able to tell who they are. In the case of agent 007 James Bond everybody knows who he is. He can walk into any bar in the world. The barman will say "Ahh! Mr Bond we've been expecting you". The barman will then proceed to pour James Bond his favourite cocktail, shaken and not stirred. So what does a spy really look like? If you look at an audience in the theatre or observe people at a bus stop or in a crowd that's exactly what spies look like. Like you and me ordinary everyday people. We will be looking at some ordinary people of the 1940s who played such an important role spying supposedly for the Germans but feeding them so much disinformation that it helped to form the foundations of what led to Operation Overlord that had such a successful outcome.

The year is 1943, the Battle of the Atlantic is slowly being won. Up to now we had been losing the war. The German U-boats were sinking more of our merchant vessels then we were able to replace. In 1942 Britain needed to import 75% of its food and 95% of its oil to survive. But only a fraction of this was being achieved; by that August Britain had six weeks supplies of food left. Food rationing was at its height. By late

1942 we had suffered the heaviest losses of merchant shipping in the war, 5.5 million tons in just ten months. The Bletchley Park code-breakers had just got back into the U-boat code "shark" which we had not been able to break since February 1942. We could not afford to lose the code again. We were sinking U-boat at a higher frequency than ever before. We had to protect Ultra, which was the output product of Bletchley Park. Ultra was being used by the Royal air force with the help of Air to Surface Vessel radar (ASV) to locate U-boats and sink them. This was now more efficient than ever.

In early 1943 Winston Churchill and President Roosevelt had a meeting in Casablanca. It was time to discuss the war's end game. At this meeting tentative plans were made how the Allies would invade and liberate Europe and rid it of the Nazi regime. Later that year another meeting was held at Tehran where Churchill, Roosevelt and Stalin discussed the different options for diversionary plans. The general invasion was almost certainly going to be on the Normandy beaches but we had to make the Germans believe it was going to be elsewhere. Hitler knew that sooner or later the allies would attempt some kind of invasion, he also knew there would be a diversionary raid. So the plan was to organise many diversions to really confuse the Germans. This would involve very subtle and totally select planning. Winston Churchill said "this whole affair must be protected by a bodyguard of lies".

One of the ways which was used to protect Ultra-intelligence and avoid the Germans thinking we had compromised the Enigma code was due to Eddie Chapman

British double agent Zigzag. Through his German spymaster, he had convinced Admiral Karl Doenitz, commander of the U-boats, that the British had a new secret weapon. Agent Zigzag's contacts supplied the Germans with the fake plans and information. This certainly helped the situation as by May 1943 Admiral Doenitz had lost over 100 U-boats. Owing to these severe losses Doenitz decided that it was time to remove the U-boats from the North Atlantic. Now the North Atlantic was becoming a safer place it was time to start bringing equipment and personnel from the United States for the largest invasion that the world has ever known, "Operation Overlord" the reclaiming of Europe. This is just one example how the disinformation passed to the Germans from a double agent changed the course of the war.

The overall diversion plan was called "Operation Bodyguard." The plans for this would be made by the London controlling section, made up of a committee of top military personnel from all the services including MI5 and MI6 and also members of the war cabinet. The British intelligence services would play a major role in this deception planning operation. It is MI5 who are responsible for home security and defence of the realm while MI6 looked at threats from overseas, deploying agents in foreign lands. The wireless intercept service was also involved (Y Service), this was our ears on Europe, intercepting enemy messages. Bletchley Park would be deciphering the coded signals from the Y-stations then passing them on to the British military Headquarters. The radio security service MI8c, (RSS) was initially run jointly by the General Post Office (GPO) and MI5 and later by MI6. They were listening out for clandestine radio transmissions within Britain assisted by hundreds of amateur radio operators who acted as voluntary interceptors (VI's). The most important help that we had, came from the German defence agency itself, known as the Abwehr.

The Abwehr

Abwehr literally means defence. It was inaugurated in 1921 under the German military intelligence as a counter espionage organization which existed until 1945. Despite the fact the Treaty of Versailles did not allow for the establishment of a German intelligence organization as such, it did allow for the defence against foreign espionage, the *Abwehr's* role evolved considerably over time.

The name used for the German military between the wars was *Reichswehr,* the military organization of the *Weimar Republic.* The first head was Major Friedrich Gempp, a former deputy to Col. Walther Nicolai, the head of German intelligence during World War I. In the early days it composed of three officers and seven former officers plus a clerical staff. By the 1920s it was organized into three sections:

I. Reconnaissance

II. Code breaking and Radio Monitoring

III. Counterespionage

The *Reichsmarine* (German Navy) intelligence staff merged with the *Abwehr* in 1928. In the 1930s, with the rise of the Nazi movement, the German Ministry of Defence was reorganized; surprisingly, on June 7, 1932, a naval officer, Capt. Konrad Patzig, was named chief of the *Abwehr*, despite the fact that it was staffed largely by Army officers. But perhaps not surprisingly, due to the small size of the organization and its limited importance at that time, it was unsuitable for a more ambitious Army officer. Another possible factor was that naval officers had more foreign experience than their Army counterparts and understood more of foreign affairs. However, all three services eventually developed their own intelligence staff.

Admiral Wilhelm Franz Canaris born in 1887, who had worked as an intelligence officer in the Imperial German Navy on-board the light cruiser Dresden during the First World War, became the commanding officer of the battleship *Schlesien*. After Hitler came to power Canaris was put in charge of the *Abwehr*, in January 1935.

The *Abwehr* dramatically increased in strength within a short time. Each *Abwehr* station throughout Germany was based on military (army) districts. More offices were opened in amenable neutral countries and in the occupied territories as the greater Reich expanded. Just as an example of the size of the organisation, the *Abwehr*'s intelligence organisation in Madrid alone was an extraordinary 87 personnel directly attached to the German embassy, along with a further 228 intelligence staff, a total of 315. This contingent was believed to control no fewer than 1500 senior agents spread throughout Spain, headed by Commander. Gustav Leinster. This remarkable network produced such a volume of information that some 34 wireless operators and 10 cipher clerks were required to handle the radio traffic. It was sufficiently important in the German intelligence machine to keep up the hourly wireless schedule with the *Abwehr* relay station near Wiesbaden.

When the *Abwehr* sent a message to their regional office it was collated and sent through to the *Abwehr* Secret Intelligence Service radio Office the *Kupferhof 'Ausland Abwehr Funkstelle* Wohldorf north of Hamburg. Then it was forwarded to FHW *fremde heere der Wehrmacht* (foreign armies intelligence service) located at 76/78 Tirpitzufer, Berlin, headed by Alexis Roenne, a close confidante of Adolf Hitler. These were the collators of all intelligence. Their offices were adjacent to the offices of the OKW, the *oberkommando der Wehrmacht*, Headed by Generalfeldmarschall Wilhelm Keitel, then passed onto the desk of Adolf Hitler.

The *Abwehr* would send spies to Britain. They would be either dropped in by parachute into a remote field somewhere or they would be put off a boat or submarine close to the British coast, into a dinghy, then row to shore to a remote cove. Spies also came into Britain posing as one of the many refugees escaping Nazi Germany. Once in Britain the spy would find a hidden area and make radio contact with their German case officers. Their message would be converted into a hand cipher stating their safe arrival. The radio was supplied with plug-in crystals that were tuned to a fixed frequency. A specific time would have been allocated to transmit the message. The spy's message was then received by the *Abwehr* case officers who would possibly be in Paris, Madrid, Lisbon or even Oslo. The message would be checked then converted into an unreadable cipher using the G type Enigma machine, then sent on by radio Morse code. This would be received at *Abwehr* radio headquarters in Hamburg. Eventually this was forwarded on to Berlin.

Soon as the German spies in Britain made their first radio transmission it was quickly intercepted by our radio security service, through either the voluntary interceptors or by our direction finding systems. Spies were tracked down very quickly and arrested. The Radio Security Service (RSS) was originally set up by Ralph Sheldon Mansfield, 4th Baron Sandhurst. Lord Sandhurst who had been in the signal service in World War I and an amateur radio operator, (radio ham) and Arthur Watts a member of British naval intelligence, similarly a keen radio amateur who happened to be president of the Radio Society of Great Britain. The historian Hugh Trevor Roper (later Lord Dacre) an expert in the German language was also working for the organisation. The RSS would be initially located in dingy offices accommodated in spare cells at Wormwood Scrubs prison in West London. As the war progressed they moved to a safe haven outside London at Arkley View in Barnet Hertfordshire. This was a large house with a row of typical temporary government huts in the rear garden. The RSS headquarters in Barnet was simply known as PO Box 25 Barnet.

It was soon realised that the handful of intercept stations around the country sending their messages to PO Box 25 were grossly insufficient for the amount of radio traffic coming across the airways. Arthur Watts approached the Radio Society of Great Britain (RSGB), to contact thousands of their members who were amateur radio operators whose radio transmitters were confiscated at the commencement of the war. The radio hams were allowed to keep their radio receiving equipment. Where operators were not of military age or were disabled, they were contacted and asked to become voluntary interceptors (VI's). They were thoroughly checked out and had to sign the Official Secrets Act. Their job would be to scan the airways searching for unexplained radio transmissions normally in code. Once located the details would be entered on a RSS log sheet and sent by post to PO Box 25 Barnet.

At Arkley View they would collate all the information. It would be sent through to Bletchley Park for messages to be deciphered and directed onto MI5. PO Box 25 was now receiving thousands of messages every day, most of them legitimate commercial messages, very few seem to be coming from possible German agents. But the voluntary interceptors were picking up some strange coded messages coming from the continent. These were in groups of five letters, seeming to look like amateur radio signals coming from abroad. At Arkley View these messages were being collated then sent to Bletchley Park. It would seem that these messages were coming from the *Abwehr* preparing to send agents to Britain. It appeared that some of the staff at Barnet including Hugh Trevor Roper were attempting to decode the messages themselves. This practice was immediately made illegal as this could undermine the whole security operation.

A further complication of security was established when the Daily Mail printed on 4 February 1941 with an article headed "Spies tap into Nazi codes", this could have been picked up by the Germans as they read British newspapers for any snippets of information. However it looks as if it was missed.

PO Box 25 at this time was date and you completely run by MI5 and grew out of its efficiency due to high levels of incoming work. To maintain further security an approach was made by Admiral Hugh Sinclair chief of MI6 to Colonel Richard Gambier Parry, head of MI6 communications. He was asked to set up a new intercept station for the RSS (MI8) in North Buckinghamshire just 10 miles north of Bletchley Park at Hanslope Park. This became known as special communications unit three (SCU3) from June 1941 the Radio Security Service MI8 became MI8(c) and was completely controlled by MI6. Gambier Parry was also responsible for Whaddon Hall 4 miles to the west of Bletchley Park known as SCU1 where disseminated Ultra signals from Bletchley Park were forwarded by radio to our commanders abroad.

Bletchley Park, home of the Government Code and Cipher School, had many functions in wartime signals intelligence, hence the 10,000 staff that eventually worked for the establishment. One of the code-breaker's tasks was to break into the German spy network. There are two sides to this operation. The radio security service now at Hanslope Park will pass the intercepted signals from the German agents that were being prepared to be sent to Britain. These messages will now be sent to RSS at Arkley View (PO Box 25) for registration and analysis of direction finding (D/F) then forwarded onto Bletchley Park for code breaking. The enemy agent would have been signalling to their case officers or controller in Lisbon or Madrid, using a hand cipher stating when and where they would be arriving in Britain. This code was broken by Oliver Strachey at Bletchley Park, a veteran code-breaker from World War I's military section MI1b. This information was passed to MI5 this message would reveal where the enemy agent is to be located, where he is going, what he has observed, also when he will make his next radio transmission. This information was passed to MI5 which enabled them to quickly locate and arrest the spy.

The next part of the communication received by the spymaster or controller in Lisbon, Madrid etc. would send the message received from the German agent in or about to arrive in the Britain to the *Abwehr* radio headquarters in Hamburg. To send this message the information would be encoded on to the Enigma cipher machine. These signals were intercepted by our wireless intercept "Y" stations, located mainly around the coast of Britain. Signals went directly to Bletchley Park's Registry to be sorted then passed to the relevant code-breaking department. Alfred Dillwyn Knox (Dilly Knox), the chief code-breaker, was a veteran code-breaker from World War 1. He worked for Naval Intelligence Department 25 at Room 40 at the Old Admiralty buildings in London. Now at Bletchley Park, Knox had broken the *Abwehr* Enigma early in the war which gave MI5 a deep insight to the complete workings of the German defence agency.

As soon as German agents were located, a welcoming party from the police and MI5 made an arrest very quickly.

Camp 020 was the interrogation camp for all German agents arrested as spies or who volunteered their services as a German spy working for Britain as a double agent. Camp 020 was situated at Latchmere house at Ham close to Richmond in Surrey. The camp commandant was Lt Col Robin Stevens. His methods of interrogation were never violent. He could stare at the suspect with such ferocity that they would speak quite freely, terrified as to what their fate would be. Stevens was known as "tin eye Stevens" owing to a glass monocle, it has been said he wore day and night and was known to put the fear of God into his prisoners.

German agents fell into three main categories: stupid, loyal, or mercenary. The stupid spy was badly selected by the *Abwehr*. He had no chance of surviving in this environment and was probably forced into spying through some kind of threat, once identified was put into prison for the rest of the war. If the spy was a loyal supporter of Hitler and the Nazi regime they would be tried and executed. Then you had the mercenary. These did it for the money, the lifestyle, the buzz, and the sheer thrill of being a spy. These were the most important to us as we would possibly turn these spies to work for Britain. If they were clever they could be paid by the *Abwehr* and also MI5. These were known as double-agents. This situation caused an issue in our security services. Up until now, German spies were dealt with by MI5, who were responsible for home security. Spies who were to act as our own agents became the responsibility of MI6, the organisation which dealt with our agents overseas. So after major discussions, it was decided that a new sub-organisation of MI5 would be created.

Control of the new double agents fell to Thomas Argyll Robertson, a charismatic MI5 agent. A Scot and something of a playboy, Robertson had some early experience with double agents; just prior to the war he had been case officer to Arthur Owens (code name Snow). Owens was an oddity and it became apparent that he was playing off the Germans and British, although to what end Robertson was unable to discover. The experiment had not appeared to be a success but MI5 had learned lessons about how *Abwehr* operated and how double agents might be useful. Robertson believed that turning German spies would have numerous benefits, disclosing what information the *Abwehr* wanted and to mislead them as part of a military deception. It would also discourage them from sending more agents, if they believed an operational network existed. Section B1a (a subordinate of B section, under Guy Liddell) was formed and Robertson was put in charge of handling the double-agent program.

Robertson's first agents were not a success. Giraffe (George Graf) was never really used also Gander (Kurt Goose). (MI5 had a fondness for amusingly relevant code names), had been sent to Britain with a radio that could only transmit and both were quickly decommissioned. The next two attempts were even more farcical; Gösta Caroli and Wulf Schmidt (a Danish citizen) landed, via parachute, in September 1940. The two were genuine Nazis, had trained together and were friends. Caroli was coerced into turning double in return for Schmidt's life being spared, whilst Schmidt was told that Caroli had sold him out and in anger swapped sides.

Caroli quickly became a problem, he attempted to strangle his MI5 case officers before making an escape, carrying a canoe on a motorcycle. He vaguely planned to row to Holland but came unstuck after falling off the bike in front of a policeman. He was eventually recaptured and judged too much trouble to be used. Schmidt was more of a success; codenamed 'Tate', he continued to contact Germany until May 1945. These eccentric spies made Robertson aware that handling double agents was going to be a difficult task.

MI5 B1a

At MI5 department B1a was set up to allow the control of double agents. A working group was to be chaired by John Cecil Marsterman (an Oxford don, and writer of thrillers). Masterman was educated at the Royal Naval Colleges of Osborne and Dartmouth, at Worcester College, Oxford, where he read modern history. He studied at the University of Freiburg where he also was an exchange lecturer in 1914, at the outbreak of World War I. As a result, he was interned as an enemy alien for four years in a detention camp in Ruhleben. During his internment, Masterman took the opportunity to further polish his German. After his return from captivity, Masterman became tutor of Modern History at Christ Church, Oxford, where he was also censor (1920–26). In the 1920s he became a notable player of cricket, tennis and hockey, participating in international competitions, and in 1931 he toured Canada with the

Marylebone Cricket Club; he was acknowledged as a master gamesman in Stephen Potter's book Gamesmanship. After World War II he returned to Oxford, becoming Provost of Worcester College (1946–61) and Vice-Chancellor of Oxford University during 1957 and 1958. Masterman was knighted for his services in 1959.

The Twenty Committee was named after the two crosses (double cross) representing the Roman twenty "XX". They met once a week at 58 St James's St London SW1. MI5 Department B1a was now responsible for all Double Cross activities. Enemy spies arriving in Britain, were equipped with the following: radio transmitter, invisible ink, code-book, revolver, wad of cash and a capsule containing Potassium Cyanide and a questionnaire. The questionnaire consisted of a list of what the Germans wanted their spy to find out, and to send the information back to them by radio or letter written with secret invisible ink. This information could be regarding the sighting and whereabouts of troops, information about dockyards or factories, even the problems caused by bomb damage or public opinion. So once a spy was caught, and providing he was suitable as a double agent, he needed to respond to the Germans' questionnaire. So this was our opportunity to give false information to the Germans. It obviously had to be a very subtle operation so not to cause the Germans to believe that their agent was being controlled by the British.

Yet another department was set up. Known as the wireless board "W Board", it would create the information that we wanted the Germans to believe. Its input came from the military and our security services. To give it the air of authenticity the W Board would add to the fabrication some real information that would be harmless for the enemy to have. This was known as "Chicken feed", the double agent would then send that information back to their *Abwehr* case officers using their radio set. The message was sent using the *Abwehr* hand cipher, at a precise time and from the agent's location normally, from a MI5 safe house. You could of course ask "how did we know if the agent is sending the exact message that we ordered them to send?" as they may be acting as a triple agent. Or it's possible that the spy was given a secret control character to send within the message that would indicate that the agent was being controlled by the British. What the agent did not know and was not going to find out was that not only was their radio transmission monitored between London and their handling agents, it was also being tracked from the handling agents to *Abwehr* HQ in Hamburg. So we knew that the Germans were trusting all of the information we were sending them, which was believed whole heartedly right to the very top of the Third Reich. This was one of the principals of how the deception plans for D Day was to be formulated.

I have chosen five spies who were key in delivering the main source of fabricated chicken feed, which went to the very top of the German command. This information strengthened the deception plans that the allies were intent on using for the invasion of Europe, hoping once and for all to rid Europe of the Nazi menace. These five spies, for one reason or another volunteered their services to British Intelligence while pretending to work for the Germans. One mistake would have cost their and possibly their families lives, and could have blown the plan for D-Day, delaying victory for years, at a terrible cost.

Dusko Popov

Was the Yugoslavian son of a wealthy businessman with contacts in high places. Popov studied at Freiburg University. Whilst there, he had a friend who like himself, was also wealthy, Johnny Jebsen. One day, Popov was out with his girlfriend in a restaurant, when the Gestapo arrested them both. Unknown to Popov, she was being followed, he was unaware that she was an active Communist. The result being they were both thrown in gaol. Popov was treated badly. Through his father's personal business contacts with Herman Goering, Popov was released, but always maintained a hatred of the Nazis.

Some years later, his old friend from University, Johnny Jebsen made contact and they agreed to meet up in a restaurant in Belgrade. Jebsen put a proposition to Popov: "How would you like to make some money and have some fun?" Jebsen continued "I work for the German Defence agency, the *Abwehr*. If you become my agent, we can both make some money." Popov agreed, that he would be prepared to spy for Germany (he was lying) probably for the fun more than the money. Jebsen arranged for Popov to go to Lisbon and meet up with Kramer von Auenrode alias Ludovico von Karsthoff, who was to become Popov's German case officer. But prior to his journey and after his meeting with Johnny Jebsen, Popov decided to contact the British Embassy in Belgrade. He was put in touch with an agent who took notes and made special arrangements. Popov was then advised to continue with his contact in Lisbon. Once in neutral Lisbon, he would be able to travel to Britain which was relatively easy, as there were reasonably regular flights. After his meeting in Lisbon with von Karsthoff, where he was trained in the art of spying, he was sent to England. Von Karsthoff gave him money, a questionnaire, and eventually a radio set, this was Popov's license to have a great time at the expense of the Nazis. Popov arrived at the Whitchurch airport Bristol in December 1940.

As soon as Popov arrived in England he was waved through by customs officers who had been briefed of his arrival. He was met by Jock Horsfall a pre-war racing driver now working for MI5 and was rushed to central London where he would see the results of the Blitz and the bombed out buildings. He checked into the Savoy Hotel in the Strand. It was there that he made contact with the security services who had been tipped off by Belgrade. This is where he had an initial meeting with TAR Robertson. After several days of questions and interrogation TAR was satisfied with Popov's authenticity and he was given the temporary codename of Skoot. Popov was to operate under the control of MI5 dept. B1a. He was allocated a case officer, Billy Lake. Popov's questionnaire from the Germans was given to the "W" board to fabricate answers to be sent to the enemy. The information would be sent to von Karsthoff by mail, written in invisible secret ink. Popov would be sent money in return, as well as another questionnaire. Money and future questionnaires were usually sent to foreign agents (double agents) via the diplomatic bags of neutral or non-aggressive countries.

As far as Popov was concerned, "Let the good times roll!" Gambling, booze, girls and fun fun fun! Yes, all this in the middle of World War II. After some time of hoodwinking the enemy, there came an order from the Germans. As Popov was so successful in Britain, sending all this reliable although notional information back to Germany, he was to be sent to the USA to structure a similar kind of operation. The orders involved setting up a network of agents. Popov was not too happy about this as he was having such a great time. British Intelligence suggested that if he did not go, they may suspect that he was being controlled by the British. MI5 B1a contacted the FBI which was run by J. Edgar Hoover. Hoover did not want any German spies in America. He said "the only thing we do with German spies is shoot them." But orders came from above and in August 1941, Popov travelled to USA to spy for the Germans.

When Popov arrived in New York 12th of August 1941 he checked into the Waldorf Astoria Hotel on New York's Park Avenue. Popov's first job would be to view the questions that the Germans had supplied him. His questions were hidden on a sheet of typed paper. Several of the sentences finished with a full stop. The full stop was in fact a micro dot a new type of technology that the Germans had just developed. Popov had to go out and buy a microscope to read the documents. The German's were very keen to know about bases in Hawaii and especially Pearl Harbour. They want to know about naval formations, transport depots, mine depots, submarine sections, workshops, aerodromes, petrol depots, underground installations, a floating dock, they also wanted reports regarding the number of aircraft hangers; in fact they wanted to know just about absolutely everything.

This information was sent onto J. Edgar Hoover via MI5, but either this was not taken seriously or was not passed on. Part of Adolf Hitler's masterplan was to include Japan as part of his world domination. He kept close ties with Tokyo through the Japanese ambassador to Nazi Germany, Hiroshi Oshima. Just five months later, in December 1941, Japan attacked Pearl Harbour causing untold damage, which resulted in bringing the US into the war just four days later. So it shows that the Americans were forewarned but did nothing. For Popov, once again, it was business as usual, time to have more fun with Hitler's money; it was spend spend spend! When he ran out of money, he asked the Germans for more cash, which they sent. The Germans were sending Popov money with a scheme planned by British intelligence and himself. The plan was called Operation Midas which involved a Jewish British theatrical owner who in theory wanted to take money out of the country into the US. The Germans were told of the plan and they agreed. Of course the whole plan was a scam to get money out of the Germans and it worked. Eventually the Germans refused to send any more money, Popov borrowed and ran up massive debts. He gambled, had many girlfriends, including the famous film star Simone Simon. He bought expensive motor cars, and made himself a playboy, a menace and a nuisance. Hoover was fed up hearing about his escapades, and ordered him out of the country or "he would have him arrested, charged under the Man Act and thrown in jail".

Popov returned to Lisbon. On his return von Karsthoff was not well pleased and ordered Popov to attend a meeting so that he could question him on why the USA operation failed to produce any new agents. Popov immediately took an offensive position by blaming the Germans for not sending him enough money, and wasting his valuable time by under-funding the operation. Popov said, "I have a good mind to resign over your failure to finance the operation correctly". Now, Popov was not stupid, he knew that a lot of the monies coming from the Germans for their agents like himself was being creamed off by case officers such as von Karsthoff. He found this out from his friend Johny Jebsen, who was always on the fiddle. If von Karsthoff was caught creaming off agents' money, he would be sent to Berlin, interviewed by the Gestapo then if lucky, sent the Russian Front! So Popov got an immediate apology from von Karsthoff who then asked if he could possibly return to England to carry on where he left off. Of course, this was accepted.

Popov's friend Johny Jebsen came to a sticky end. He was always sailing close to the wind, getting involved in finance deals and smuggling money. It was only a matter of time before the Gestapo caught up with him. Von Karsthoff advised him to go to Berlin to be interviewed by the authorities. He refused on several occasions, and was just about to change his allegiance and start working for MI5 when he was duped to return to Lisbon where he was told he was to be awarded an Iron Cross. But when he entered the building he was gagged knocked out and smuggled to Germany in the back of a car. Johnny Jebsen was never seen again. Dusko Popov continued his "work" with MI5 B1a. Dusko Popov became known as MI5 agent "Tricycle" (due to an apparent preference for three in a bed), he becomes our first D-day spy. Also Popov's brother was engaged as a double agent working for Britain. An interesting fact was the Germans knew Dusko Popov as agent Ivan. The real name of Popov's brother who works MI5 was Ivo Popov. His MI5 codename was Dreadnought.

Roman Czerniawski

Was a Polish Air force Officer and a hero. In 1940 he volunteered for allied espionage work in France. One day in a café in a quiet street in Paris just by chance he met up with Mathilde Carre. Mathilde also hated the Nazis and together they decided to do something about it. They recruited agents for an organisation which they named "*Interallie*" (Allied). They were supplying information to the French resistance groups from their office in Montmartre in Paris. Their brilliant communications system involved placing messages in the toilets of railway coaches, by unscrewing the mirrors and placing the message behind. They became very successful with many agents all over France. One day, when he returned to the office, Czerniawski thought he recognised a man walking past him. It happened to be Hugo Bleicher of the *Abwehr*, who was working on behalf of the Gestapo. The next thing they knew, on the 17th November 1941, was that the building was raided by the Gestapo. All the staff at "*Interallie*" were arrested, and all their records were confiscated. The offices were trashed, and all the staff, including Czerniawski and Carre were arrested and thrown in a terrible Gestapo prison in Paris. Czerniawski as you can imagine was very badly treated, and was interrogated several times. On one occasion he was taken from his cell, and thought that he was going to be shot, but he was interrogated again, this time by a member of the *Abwehr*. Hugo Ernst Bleicher who was a senior non-commissioned officer of Nazi Germany who worked against French Resistance in German-occupied France. He was quite impressed with how Czerniawski had set up the organisation "*Interallie*".

The *Abwehr* gave him an option to set up as their agent in England and recruit more spies to work for the Germans and of course as he was Polish he could be accepted in Britain. The offer was one of those that he was unable to refuse. In other words, he would have to work as a spy for the Germans or be executed by them. Czerniawski agreed to spy for the *Abwehr* as it was his "get out of gaol free card". There was one caveat: The Germans made it clear that, in case he was thinking of double-crossing them, they knew where his family lived in Poland, and they would be in great peril. Roman Cziernaiwski was sent to England as a German agent. He immediately made his way to the Polish Embassy and was treated like a hero. He was then put in touch with the British Intelligence Services, and sent to camp 020 Latchmere House for interrogation by Colonel Robin Stevens, then handed over to MI5 B1a, and became our second D-day spy. Roman Czerniawski's code-name was "Brutus", as he was to stab Germany in the back.

Nathalie "Lily" Sergueiew

Was born in St Petersburg, Russia in 1912. She escaped the Russian revolution in 1917, and reached France with her family. Lily was educated in Paris, trained as a journalist and could speak fluent English and German. During 1930, she travelled throughout Germany, interviewing top Nazis such as Herman Goering. In 1937, Lily was approached to work for German Intelligence. In this instance, she refused. After the fall of France in May 1940, she agreed to work for the *Abwehr*. Her case officer was Emil Kliemann. Major Emile Kliemann was having a most delightful war. Occupied Paris was an exceptionally pleasant place to be, if you happened to sympathise with the Nazis. He had an office on the Champs-Élysées, and a comfortable apartment near the Bois de Boulogne.

Kliemann was two hours late for their rendezvous at the Café du Rond-Point. The young woman waiting at the corner table was goodlooking without being beautiful. In fluent German, Lily Sergeyev explained that she was a journalist and painter. Lily was intrigued, intelligent, and most important, interested in Kliemann. He invited her to dinner at the Cascade restaurant, near the Bois de Boulogne. The young woman insisted on bringing her dog, a small white male terrier-poodle cross named Babs, to which she was obviously devoted. Emil Kliemann trained Lily in intelligence techniques such as writing in secret ink, information gathering, and communications.

In May 1943, Lily travelled to Spain. She travelled everywhere with her beloved little dog. When Lily arrived in Madrid, she contacted British Intelligence at the passport office of the British embassy. British Embassy passport offices were nearly always a cover for MI6 to base their agents. Lily offered her services to British Intelligence. They accepted her and she was initially sent to Gibraltar to await transport to Britain. The authorities would not allow her to take her little dog with her due to the strict quarantine rules in the UK. Lily was very upset over this, but she was promised that they would look after the dog, and it would follow later. When she arrived in Britain, she was taken eventually to Rugby Mansions in Kensington, west London, where TAR Robertson interviewed her and introduced Lily to her British case officer Mary Shearer. What Lily was not aware of that her house-keeper, A Yugoslavian woman Maritza, was an MI5 agent "Snark", keeping an eye on Lily and reporting back on her movements.

Lily started sending back information to Germany as Kliemann had provided her with a questionnaire. But Lily was depressed and became difficult for MI5 to control her. She was missing her dog badly and kept asking when it would arrive in England. The answer was always the same: soon. Lily continued to meet Kliemann by travelling back and forth to Lisbon, bringing back further questionnaires, but still no dog. Lily was becoming even more depressed, then a telegram from Gibraltar. "Your dog was sent to a kennel in Algiers and by complete accident it escaped from its cage and ran into a road, and was run over. We are very sorry". Lily was convinced that the British killed her dog, and she wanted revenge. Lily was distraught and took it upon herself to make an arrangement with Kliemann that should she become controlled by the British, she would send certain hidden characters in her messages. This would have indicated that Lily was sending false information back to the *Abwehr*, which of course, she was. The information about the false character should have immediately been reported to MI5, but Lily kept it to herself so she could get revenge for the loss of her dog at any time. Though she often thought about using it Lily never used the control signal to alert the Germans that she was being controlled by the British. She revealed her secret by chance to MI5, and they were livid that she was sitting on a time bomb. At any moment she could have wrecked the complete Double Cross system along with all the D-day planning. Lily was used for the build up to D-day, passing false information back to the Germans. But after D-day, she was sacked from MI5. But MI5 were still sending the Germans false information pretending it was coming from Lily Sergeyev. Her code-name was "Treasure" because she really was, (but at most times to MI5 she was a pain). Lily became our third D-day spy.

Elvira de la Fuente Chaudior

Was the daughter of a very wealthy Peruvian. She was living in Paris where she had spent most of her upbringing. Her father became Peruvian charge d'affair to the Vichy government. Elvira got bored with everything she did in life. She even got married to a very wealthy businessman and got bored with him and divorced. She moved to England and continued her high life there, frequenting the night-clubs and gambling casinos, where she always lost money. She could often be seen at Crockfords or Hamiltons Club in London's fashionable Mayfair. But eventually she ran out of money. One night at Hamiltons, she was pouring out her misery over a Bronx cocktail to the sympathetic ear of an RAF officer. Elvira explained how bored she was, and now with no money. The RAF officer advised her that he could put her in touch with British Intelligence, where she could possibly find work and certainly not get bored. Elvira agreed and she was put in touch with Claude Dansey, (codename Z) the deputy Head of MI6, also with Duff Cooper, the Minister of Information.

There was an initial meeting set up at the Connaught Hotel in Mayfair. With her father's diplomatic status, it was relatively easy for Elvira to travel to and from Vichy France. The Southern part of France which after the German invasion of May 1940 remained under French control. In charge of the Vichy Government was Philip Petain, a French WW1 hero, but now unfortunately just a puppet for the Nazis until he capitulated in November 1942. Elvira eventually got to France under the control of MI5 to continue her gambling in the exclusive clubs and casinos in Paris. She was still losing money big time, but now it was MI5's money going around the roulette tables and down the drain. It was in one of these casinos that a friend of a friend put her in touch with someone who could provide Elvira with the money that she needed to throw at the tables. This someone happened to be Helmut Bleil, a freelance agent working as an *Abwehr* recruiting officer looking out for new agents. Bleil gave Elvira the rundown of what would be expected of her, how she would have to go to Britain with a questionnaire and provide the Germans with information. Elvira was trained in communications, how to write letters in secret ink, and how to operate a radio transmitter. Bleil made it quite clear to Elvira that if she cheated on the Germans, it would cost her her life. Her German code-name was "Dorette". Bliel then handed Elvira a bottle of secret ink. As she put it in her handbag, she prayed that it would not clink on the other bottle of secret ink that MI5 had given her. Elvira made her way to Britain to work for MI5 B1a, her case officer was Hugh Astor. It would add the thrill to her life that she desperately needed as she became Britain's fourth D-day spy, code-named "Bronx", the name of her favourite cocktail.

Bronx Cocktail Recipe

1 ½ ounces gin,

¼ ounce dry vermouth,

¼ ounce sweet vermouth,

1 ounce orange juice,

Orange slice for garnish.

Shaken not stirred

Juan Pujol Garcia

In Spain it is traditional to take the father's surname after the Christian name and the mother's surname last. So as far as we are concerned he will be called Pujol. Pujol was not just a Catalonian chicken farmer, he had many jobs. He also served the army in the Spanish Civil war. He claimed to have fought on both sides without ever firing a bullet. He hated war, he hated the communists, and equally hated the Fascists. When World War II broke out, Spain remained neutral, but it leaned heavily on the side of Germany with an incredible network of active *Abwehr* agents. Pujol could see the Fascists, as in the Nazis, on the move again. He wanted to do anything he could to help the allies.

In January 1941 Pujol made contact with the British Embassy in Madrid. He attempted to offer his services to the British Intelligence as he believed that he could travel relatively freely being a respected businessman. However, after several approaches he was sent from clerk to clerk from pillar to post. He then was told to put his requests in writing, as they were for too busy to see him. He was then sent away empty-handed. After this frustrating episode Pujol was wondering what his next step could possibly be. He then figured out that if he could contact the German intelligence service, he could supply them with false information. This he thought would be his contribution to helping the allies.

Pujol's next call was to the German Embassy where he asked to be put through to the attaché, a similar scenario was to follow. He was told we are very busy today and suggested that he wrote in. Pujol then told the Spanish clerk that he had intelligence information for them. There was a pause; the clerk then asked Pujol to call back the following morning when he was told to go to café Lyon at 4.40pm the next day where a man called Fredrico, alias Friedrich Knappe-Ratey, stationed in Madrid would meet him. After several meetings Pujol would be working for the Office of the Madrid *Abwehr*, which was originally set up in 1937 and controlled by Gustav Leisner the head of the Madrid section. He told them that he was able to go to England and spy for the Germans. They said that it was a good idea as they waved goodbye to him. Before he left he asked for expenses to take him to England. They told him "Bring us back the information and then we will pay you" It seemed as if he was not taken seriously and once again he was given the cold shoulder.

Pujol left their office feeling dejected. A few days later he returned to the *Abwehr* office to play a very dangerous game with the Germans. He told them that he had come up with a plan. He showed them that he had been given a diplomatic visa by the Spanish authorities (this was a forgery) as they wanted him to go to England as an honorary Spanish attaché. This would enable him to travel freely to Britain and act as a German agent. Pujol also told the *Abwehr* that he knew a KLM pilot who for a small fee would take Pujol's reports and letters from England and deliver them to the Espirato Bank in Lisbon where there was a safe deposit box that Pujol could use. He could send a key to the German Embassy in Lisbon. This in effect would by-pass the

British censors. The *Abwehr* believed every word of his fabricated story and would pass their questionnaires and cash via the Lisbon safe deposit box. Pujol was given the code name Arabel. So who at the Madrid *Abwehr* was responsible for being taken in by all this baloney, head of section Gustav Leisner? Specialist Captain Karl-Erich Kuhlenthal? or Officer Friedrich Knapp, alias Fredrico? Whom all held senior positions in the *Abwehr*.

Pujol never had any intention of travelling to England it was all a scam. On April 6th 1941 Pujol moved to Lisbon where his family soon followed. As soon as he was settled he headed down the road to a second-hand bookshop. He bought some old English magazines and newspapers, a well-thumbed copy of the Baedeker Tourist Guide to Britain, as well as Bradshaw's Railway Time Tables. Agent "Arabel" started to fabricate reports and send them to the *Abwehr* office in Madrid via the Espirato Bank. Even Pujol was surprised when he was paid for these reports, the more he wrote, the more they paid. Pujol was virtually writing out his own cheques. This went on for many months. The *Abwehr*'s Lisbon case officer for Agent Arabel was Captain Karl-Erich Kuhlenthal. He would send this information onto *Abwehr* HQ in Hamburg and then onto the head of the Third Reich. Pujol was making big errors in his reports that the Germans never picked up on.

He was pretending to be travelling to Britain, spying for the Germans at dockyards, ports and factories. The fact was that he had never been to England and never left Lisbon. Pujol was purporting to pay a pilot for posting letters that he actually posted himself, and then pocketed the pilot's expenses, as if they came from Britain by aeroplane. He told the Germans that on his visit to Glasgow that he saw shipbuilders in cafes drinking flagons of wine. This error was never picked up by the Germans. He was also informing them of imaginary convoys leaving Liverpool for the Mediterranean, with the numbers of merchant ships and Royal Navy Convoy escort details. However, all this information was being paid for by the Germans, and then transmitted to the *Abwehr* HQ by radio, using the Enigma Cipher System. These messages were being intercepted, broken by Bletchley Park, then passed onto MI5 B1a, who were then in a bit of a quandary.

It appeared from the decrypts that there was a German agent called Arabel, operating in Britain about whom they knew nothing. The Radio Security Service (RSS) were put on full alert to listen out for signals from a German agent operating in Britain, as we believed it should not have been possible with the systems MI5 had in place. On closer inspection of the messages sent by Arabel, it just did not make sense. Army camps where there were no army camps, factories where there were no factories, and convoys of ships that just didn't exist.

What was going on? It was soon established that this information was coming via Madrid. MI6 agents were allocated to track down this mysterious spy. Eventually after several months, MI6 agent Gene Risso-Gill was able to locate agent Arabel operating from Lisbon. After interviews and interrogations, Juan Pujal Garcia and his family were secretly brought to Britain via Gibraltar. The family were taken to an

MI5 safe house at 35 Crespigny Road Cricklewood in North London.

Pujol was given the temporary codename of Bovril. After further interrogations by MI5, it was decided that, as he was such a good actor who could fool the Germans as he did so often, MI5 re-named him Garbo, after the actress Greta Garbo. He continued his work of supplying the Germans with false information. MI5 allocated him his British case officer Tommy Harris, a half Spanish art dealer who lived in Chelsea. Garbo's information was now composed for him by the W. Board (Wireless board), based on the questionnaires that the German's were sending him. So now Garbo was being paid by MI5 (although not much) as well as receiving good money from the Germans. It was not long before Garbo started recruiting agents to spy for him. Over time, he had set up a large network of agents around Britain. They included Welsh fascists, lorry drivers, an army officer, dock workers, Gibraltarians, a South African working at the Ministry of Information, employers of airlines and anti-Communists.

The Garbo network consisted of twenty-six sub-agents around the country, who all sent in intelligence reports for the Germans. The *Abwehr* in return were supplying Garbo with further questionnaires and cash to pay all of his twenty six agents and. Garbo was also claiming expenses to go around the country visiting his agents. The truth was that not one of these agents existed, Garbo with Tommy Harris had created them all out of thin air. The Germans believed every word of these reports at the highest level. On one occasion the Germans criticised one piece of information that was missing. Garbo had failed to report on a particular convoy from Liverpool. A plan to deal with this discrepancy was conjured up by Garbo and Tommy Harris and the W board. Garbo reported back that his agent in Liverpool was ill, and in hospital. On Tuesday, 4 November 1942 the Liverpool Daily Post newspaper put a notice in the column of deaths that William Maximillian Gerbers (Garbo's number two agent) after a long illness had died at the age of 59. Garbo sent this fabricated information back to the Germans, and they responded by sending money for the agent's family. Of course, the Liverpool agent, just like all the others, never existed. On another occasion Garbo even informed the Germans of a convoy leaving Liverpool, the Germans dispatched a wolf pack of U-boats to the Western approaches of Britain to intercept it. Then at a later date it was revealed that their captains were disciplined for not finding the convoy. Garbo kept up this whole masquerade going right through to the end of the war. Juan Pujal Garcia, Agent Garbo, became our fifth D-day spy.

There were other double agents who should be mentioned whose stories are quite involved. Arthur Owens agent Snow, Wulf Schmidt agent Tate. Agents Zig Zag, also Mutt & Jeff and others who risked everything to assist the allied cause.

Fall of the Abwehr

It would appear that the *Abwehr*'s staff were not the vicious nasty murderers of the Nazi type. This was true as the *Abwehr* and the Nazis never quite saw eye to eye. It has been said that the *Abwehr* suspected that their agents could possibly be fabricating and maybe even being controlled by the British. Some of the reports sent in were certainly padded out and exaggerated by the German case officers prior to being sent through to Berlin. We know this from the decrypts received at Bletchley Park, after all many Germans felt if Hitler loses the war it could only be a good thing for Germany. There was a joke circling around Germany at the time.

There was Hitler, Himmler, Goering, and Goebbels in an air raid shelter in Berlin. During an air raid the shelter received a direct hit. The shelter was blown apart who was saved?

The answer was Germany

It is also feasible that the *Abwehr* reports that were coming in were further exaggerated, as this could mean Brownie points for that particular case officer, as it would be quite difficult to disprove a lot of these reports. At the end of the day it could cause particular case officers becoming out of favour with the Nazis, owing to a lack of information. The fear for the case officers was being sent to the Russian front. But this nice cosy club, all came tumbling down.

Two *Abwehr* officers in Turkey absconded to the allies. It was thought Dr. Erich and Elisabeth Vermehren were to be investigated in Berlin by the Gestapo for allegedly spreading anti- Nazi views. They knew what could be in store for them so they decided to try and defect to the allies, they contacted the

British embassy in Ankara. It was there that Nicolas Elliot worked as an MI6 officer and head of station in Turkey. Elliot was also a long standing friend of Kim Philby, who was in those days a highly respected senior MI6 agent. Elliot assisted their escape to England via Cairo. Once in England they were housed temporarily at Kim Philby's mothers flat in Kensington. The Germans correctly believed that they took with them much top secret information. Hitler was furious; he summoned admiral Canaris the chief of the *Abwehr*. Canaris had never agreed with the Nazis, nevertheless he was promoted by them to Admiral status, to head the *Abwehr*. Canaris employed the minimum Nazi members he could get away with, to keep Heinrich Himmler at bay, as Himmler was in charge of the *Schutzstaffel* (SS) and they had their own intelligence organisation the *Sicherheitsdienst* (SD). Canaris always supported Germany as he considered himself an Admiral of the German Imperial Navy. In this instance he fell foul of Hitler and was sacked.

In the early days of his appointment Canaris was a supporter of Hitler and the National Socialist German Workers' Party (Nazis). On 18th February 1944 Hitler ordered the complete Abwehr organisation to be disbanded. It was to be replaced by the SD (*Ausland Sicherheistdeinst),* the security service for foreign countries. The SD were no pussycats, they were the intelligence services of the SS and the Nazi party. But even with the new administration in force and much of the original organisation dismantled, just enough remained in place that in many instances it was business as usual. The information

being sent by the British double cross system remained as false
as it has had ever been.

Bodyguard

Britain was now controlling the complete German Intelligence
system, with fabricated information created by the W Board to
fool the Germans. We could monitor their reaction by
intercepting and breaking their coded messages. The Germans
believed all they were told, without exception. So it was now
time to tell them about the invasion of Europe, D-day. They
knew it was coming, but they did not know where or when. This
was to be called "Operation Fortitude" the D-day deception plan.
The Germans realised that, with the impending allied invasion
of Europe, there would be some kind of deception plan involved.
What actually happened, there were to be a number of deception
plans in place. At the Tehran conference on 28th November to
1st December 1943, Churchill, Roosevelt and Stalin started to
discuss the endgame of the war, whereby plans were being made
to reclaim Europe from the Nazis. All battles must be combined
with a deception plan, so it would appear obvious to the enemy
that deception would be part of the operation. Therefore it was
decided to have numerous deception plans to confuse the enemy.
Churchill said "these plans must be protected by a bodyguard of
lies" so the overall collection of deceptions became known as
"Operation Bodyguard".

Operation Ironside was one of the deception plans which formed part of Operation Bodyguard, the invasion of Britany and Bordeaux. This was a broad strategic military deception intended to confuse the Axis high command as to Allied intentions during the lead-up to the Normandy landings. The overall aim of Bodyguard was to tie down German forces away from Normandy by threatening other targets. Ironside's specific objective was to tie up the 17th SS and 11th Panzer divisions deployed in the south of France with a seaborne operation consisting of two divisions from Britain and eight divisions direct from the USA.

Operation Fortitude North had a similar strategy to an earlier manoeuver. In 1943 Operation Cockade, consisted of a fictional field army (British Fourth Army) with its headquarters at Edinburgh Castle. It was decided to continue to use the same force during Fortitude North. Unlike its Southern counterpart the deception relied primarily on "Special Means" (information from agents) and fake radio traffic, since it was judged unlikely that German reconnaissance planes could reach Scotland un-intercepted. False information about the arrival of troops in the area was reported by double agents Mutt and Jeff, who had surrendered following their 1941 landing in the Moray Firth, while the British media cooperated by broadcasting fake information, such as football scores or wedding announcements, to non-existent troops. Fortitude North was so successful that by late spring 1944, Hitler had thirteen army divisions in Norway, including the 12th Panzer division supported by the Luftwaffe.

Operation Fortitude South was the invasion of Pas de Calais by the First United States Army Group (FUSAG) commanded by General Patton. All of these armies were completely fabricated. Whilst we were aware that the Germans wouldn't be fooled by every deception, through our network of double-cross agents, we were going to make the Germans believe in these three main possibilities. The real invasion, Operation Overlord, was planned to take place on the beaches of Normandy, meanwhile our double-cross agents would continually send messages back to the *Abwehr/SD* telling of massive troop movements where there were none and conversely where there was a build-up of troops, tanks and landing craft, we told the Germans that the roads and towns were deserted. We invented two massive armies that did not exist, "The First US army group" FUSAG, based in Kent with tens of thousands of troops ready to pounce on Calais at a moment's notice. To back-up our double-agents stories, and in case of reconnaissance flights by the Germans, we built cardboard aircraft and rubber tanks all placed in the fields of Kent. Dummy radio messages were sent day and night to show a high level of military activity. We even gave the dummy army a real-life general, General Patton.

Fortitude South, at Calais, held back the mighty 15th SS Panzer Division commanded by Field Marshall Gerd von Rundstedt and General Erwin Rommel. Operation Overlord, the real invasion at Normandy, commanded by General D Eisenhower chief of the Supreme Headquarters of the Allied Expeditionary Forces (SHAEF). Our double-cross spies were continuing to send Germany "chicken-feed", and Hitler was believing all he was told. A date was set for the 5th June 1944, but due to bad weather D-day was postponed to the 6th June. General Eisenhower insisted that it was imperative that there should be no serious opposition to the landings for at least 48 hours. Our agents were working flat-out, telling the Germans "that there will be an imminent attack on Calais at any time now".

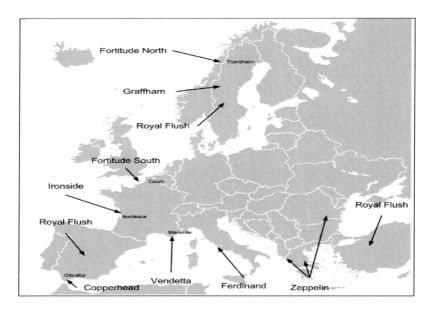

Operation Bodyguard

The invasion commenced on the Normandy beaches. Bletchley Park intercepted signals that confirmed that Hitler's general von Rundstedt and Rommel (who was away on leave at his wife's birthday on 6th June), had started to move heavy artillery south from Calais towards Normandy. This could have been an absolute disaster. On 9th June 1944 Agent Garbo sent an urgent message to the Germans: "Don't be fooled, Normandy is a diversion!" The message got to Hitler and on the same day he, ordered the 15th Panzer Division back to Calais rescinding the order to move west. Garbo and his fake agents continued to impress the Germans with his phoney information. After D+36, over a month after D-day, Hitler's generals started questioning the FUSAG invasion of Calais, but it took the Germans another four weeks to do anything about it. It was now far too late as the Expeditionary Force had now established a bridgehead, and built Mulberry harbours they were now moving inland. Hitler was now informed that the FUSAG group in Kent was now dispersing and that Normandy will be the main attack. We had to inform the Germans of this so they would keep faith in our double agents for future operations. Amazingly, Hitler was so impressed with the information that Garbo had given to the Germans he awarded Arabel (Garbo) the Iron Cross 2nd Class.

Our D-day double-cross spies laid out the playing field so that Operation Overlord could be the success that it was. As such they helped to save the lives of thousands of allied service personnel by holding back Hitler's mighty Panzers, and giving General Eisenhower not just his 48 hours, but almost six weeks. The work for our double-cross agents was not yet finished. There was to be more deception for the Germans regarding their deadliest weapons to date the V1 and V2 rockets that could have completely devastated London and other British cities. The Third Reich never found out about how gullible they were.

We were nearly caught out.

Britain was almost caught out as well. At the very heart of the British Secret Service were five Spies working for Russia. They all worked for MI5 and MI6 and one even worked at the British Government's Ultra top secret code-breaking establishment at Bletchley Park. They were all very privy to the nation's uppermost secrets, including the plans for D-day, also our double-cross system. They told the Russians everything. Of course, the Russians were then our allies, but remember that Hitler also had code-breakers. The Germans were breaking into Russian codes. The plans for Operation Overlord, D-day and the double-cross system could have been compromised through the actions of these rogues in the very highest echelons of our security services. It was an extremely close call and could have cost us the war. These highly respected individuals continued to spy for the Russians into the 1950s during the Cold War. One almost became the Chief of MI6 "C", another became the advisor of art to HM Queen Elizabeth II. These dreadful traitors were none other than Sir Anthony Blunt, Kim Philby, Guy Burgess, Donald Maclean, and John Cairncross. Burgess and Maclean defected to Moscow in 1951 following a tip-off from Philby. He defected himself in 1963. In 1979 The Prime Minister Margaret Thatcher named Sir Anthony Blunt, a former security service officer as the "fourth man" in the Cambridge spy ring.

The fifth man John Cairncross did not consider that he was a spy, he merely insisted that he was assisting the allies by passing them needed information that Stalin would not accept through normal channels. Especially that of the German decrypts of Operation Zitadelle, the battle of the Kursk. Caincross was never prosecuted for treason as it was claimed that the information at that time was passed to an ally not an enemy. John Cairncross claimed that he never spied after the war. He died October 8th 1995, in Herefordshire. I am sure we are all aware that spying goes on today in Britain, not just military spying, but also commercial infiltration of our businesses our factories, and of course the internet, sending information back to all corners of the world. It is worth remembering that most spies are not loyal to any country, they normally do it for money.

So was the *Abwehr* intelligent, dangerous and ruthless, or were they hopeless, useless and very silly indeed? There were many different sections to the *Abwehr* several were mainly administrative, the main ones are shown here.

I. Reconnaissance & Agents (mainly unbelievably stupid)

II. Cipher and Radio Monitoring (sometimes very efficient)

III. Counterespionage (normally extremely ruthless)

I think Admiral Canaris could be the answer to this. But first there is a question, why did the Germans believe that all their spies (double cross agents) were genuine? How is it possible that they were taken in by such things as a body in the sea with the Allies most secret plans in a briefcase fastened to its belt which appeared just waiting to be discovered? (Operation Mincemeat) Garbo's 26 imaginary agents to which the Germans sent regular payments, awarding agent Zigzag with an Iron Cross for not blowing up a British aircraft factory and for not destroying his British ship City of Lancaster: to believe that a complete army (FUSAG) complete with 60,000 troops was sitting waiting in Kent to attack Pas de Calais and that 50,000 troops stationed at Edinburgh Castle were waiting to attack Norway? The Germans like the British were always checking the possibility of their spies becoming triple agents. But there is an underlying factor. Without all that, D-Day may not have been a victory it was, it could have so easily become a D-Day disaster.

The war may have continued for many more years and who knows where we would be today? D-Day, correctly called Operation Overlord was a combined effort with a unique set of elements; planning, extremely brave manpower, intelligence including code breaking, photo reconnaissance and the incredible deception information passed to the Germans by our spies, to name a few. There may have been one more component that helped to make D-Day work. It could possibly have been Admiral Wilhelm Canaris himself, chief of the *Abwehr*.

Canaris became disillusioned as the atrocities that the Nazis were inflicting on the population of Poland became apparent. He became critical of the actions of the Nazi regime and complained to his superior Wilhelm Keitel. He told Keitel, that one day Germany would be held accountable for its actions.

But was told not to get involved and no account to question the actions of the Wehrmacht. But Canaris did get involved, helping several Jews to escape from Germany by making them temporary Abwehr agents, which then enabled them to escape through Switzerland. He was also involved in a plot to overthrow Hitler, He didn't agree with the Stauffenberg assassination attempt to kill Hitler, he just wanted him arrested and brought to trial. After the July 1944 plot there were many arrests, documents were seized. Canaris's name was found in documents; he was arrested and imprisoned at Flossenburg concentration camp. A bogus trial was held by SS officers at the camp and he was eventually executed in April 1945.

The day prior to his execution he tapped out a message on the cell wall in Morse code. To another prisoner captain Lunding who was once the head of intelligence in Denmark. It said "I die for my Fatherland. I have a clean conscience. I only did my duty for my country. I tried to oppose the criminal folly of Hitler, leading Germany into destruction. If you survive this please tell my wife". Canaris was probably instrumental in ensuring that no one looked too closely at some of the information from their spies and spymasters, by doing so he put a rather large dent in the wall of the Third Reich. D-Day punched a hole through that wall. After the war the SS perpetrators of his execution were brought before the Nuremberg trials. After three court sessions it could not be decided whether the actions of the SS officers was a war crime. Finally in 1956 it was seen by the court that his execution was legitimate as it was considered that Wilhelm Canaris was a traitor towards Germany.

List of released names of MI5 B1a Double agents

Artist – Johnny Jebsen

Balloon – Dickie Metcalf

Basket – Joseph Lenihan

Beetle – Petur Thomsen, based in Iceland

Biscuit – Sam McCarthy

Bootle – jointly handled by SIS and the French Deuxième Bureau

Bronx – Elvira Chaudoir

Brutus – Roman Czerniawski

Careless – Clark Korab

Carrot – (real name unknown), a Polish airman

Celery – Walter Dicketts

Charlie – Kiener, a German born in Britain

Cheese – Renato Levi, Italian Servizio Informazioni Militare agent

Cobweb – Ib Arnason Riis, based in Iceland

Dreadnought – Ivan Popov, brother of Dušan Popov, Tricycle

Dragonfly – Hans George

Father – Henri Arents

Fido – Roger Grosjean

Freak – Marquis Frano de Bona

Gander – Hans Reysen

Garbo – Juan Pujol García

Spies Lies and Double-cross Agents

Gelatine – Gerda Sullivan

Gilbert – André Latham, jointly handled by SIS and the French Deuxième Bureau

Giraffe – Georges Graf

GW – Gwilym Williams

Hamlet – Dr Koestler, an Austrian

Hatchet – Albert de Jaeger

Jacobs

Josef - Yuri Smelkov

Le Chat – Mathilde Carré

Lambert – Nikitov, a Russian

Lipstick – Josef Terradellas, a Spaniard

Meteor – Eugn Sostaric

Moonbeam – based in Canada

Mullett – Thornton, a Briton born in Belgium

Mutt and Jeff – Helge Moe and Tor Glad, two Norwegians

Peppermint – José Brugada

Puppet – Mr Fanto, a Briton

Rainbow – Günther Schütz

Rover

Scruffy – Alphonse Timmerman

Shepherd

The Snark – Maritza Mihailovic, a Yugoslavian (MI5 Safe house, house keeper)

Sniper

Snow – Arthur Owens

Spanehl – Ivan Španiel

Spider – based in Iceland

Springbok – Hans von Kotze

Stephan – Klein

Summer – Gösta Caroli

Sweet William – William Jackson

Tate – Wulf Schmidt

Teapot

Treasure – Nathalie Sergueiew (Lily Sergeyev)

Tricycle – Dušan Popov

Washout – Ernesto Simoes

Watchdog – Werner von Janowski

Weasel – A doctor, Belgian

The Worm – Stefan Zeiss

Zigzag – Eddie Chapman

Finally, spies do not all go around looking like James Bond, shaken, but not stirred.

Spies Lies and Double-cross Agents

The Enigma of the Enigma

Part 1 Background

Part 2 How Enigma works

Part 3 How the codes were broken

Part 4 How to set up your Enigma

Background

Dr Arthur Scherbius was born on 30th October 1878. He studied electricity at the Technical University Munich then went on to study at the University of Hannover, finishing in March 1903. The following year, he completed a dissertation titled "Proposal for the Construction of an Indirect Water Turbine Governor", and was awarded a doctorate in engineering (Dr.-Ing.).

Scherbius applied for a patent (filed 23 February 1918) for a cipher machine based on rotating wired wheels, what is now known as a rotor machine. Scherbius's company also purchased the rights to another patent for a rotor machine from Hugo Koch which he had patented in 1919. The machine was exhibited at the Congress of the International Postal Union in 1923 where it was offered for sale, but business was slow enough that the firm was reorganised at least twice in the 1920s.

159

The firm's cipher machine, named Enigma after the Greek *ainigma*, meaning mystery, puzzle or conundrum. The early "Enigma" machine, was initially pitched at the commercial market. There were several commercial models, and one of them was adopted by the German Navy (in a modified version) in 1926. The German Army adopted the same machine (also in a modified version somewhat different from the Navy's) a few years later. Arthur Scherbius was killed in an accident in 1929 but his invention lived on.

Rotor showing the ring clip to change the rotor turn over point *Ringstellung*

M3 German military Enigma

Courtesy Bletchley Park Trust

How Enigma works

Without the luxury of having an Enigma machine in front of you it could be a devil of a job to work out just from a text how the thing works. Of course there are many technical publications which explain every detail of each working part with every nut bolt and rivet, also don't forget the mathematical possibilities of working out the daily key. Someone once told me if I were to try every setting on a three rotor Enigma machine in the hope of finding one day's key it could take me trillions of years. Well we don't have that long so I am going to talk basics, no clever stuff and so here it is, The Enigma of the Enigma.

Some Enigma rotors used the alphabet

Bletchley Park Trust

Box containing Enigma Rotors

Bletchley Park Trust

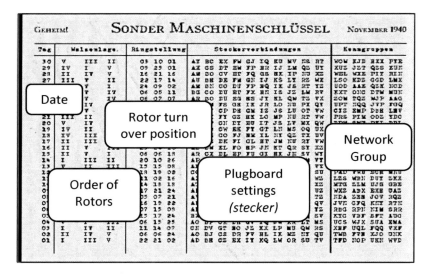

Enigma Setting Sheet *Courtesy of Bletchley Park Trust*

To explain how the Enigma machine physically operates I have put together this small straightforward example. We will assume that our sending station has set his Enigma machine from his daily setting sheet noted above.

The receiving station has also gone through the setting up procedure and the two machines are now synchronised. This procedure will be explained later.

To demonstrate how the current flows through the machine enciphering the letters we are just going to use **one** letter today to keep things as straightforward as possible.

Spies Lies and Double-cross Agents

Michael's Basic Enigma diagram

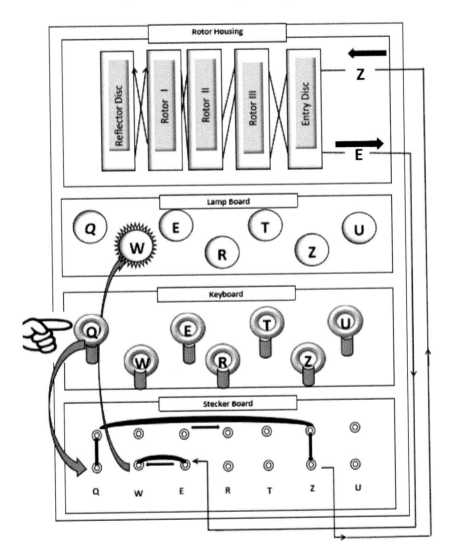

Fig.2

163

Our sending operator wishes to send just one letter **Q**. the following diagram shows the route of the letter **Q** through the Enigma's wiring configuration.

The **Q** is depressed on the keyboard. The current travels down to the plug board (*Stecker)* where a cable links **Q** to **Z**.

The **Z** now follows the path to the entry disc also at **Z**.

The current then flows through the three rotors changing letters on their way through.

The current hits the reflector disc on the left hand side and now passes back through the rotors taking a different path and leaves the entry disc as the letter **E**.

E is connected to **E** on the *Stecker* which has been linked to the letter **W**. This will now illuminate the **W** on the lamp board.

So we have enciphered plaintext letter **Q** to the cipher text letter **W**.

The letter **W** would be sent by radio Morse code (dit dah dah) to the receiving station.

One member of the three-man team will be operating the radio at the receiving station. He will write down the letter **W**, the sheet will then be passed to a second operator who will call out the letter **W** to the third Enigma operator. Providing his Enigma machine has exactly the same ground settings as the sending station he will type in the letter **W** into his Enigma keyboard and the letter **Q** which was the original plaintext will illuminate on the lamp board.

We have enciphered and deciphered the letter **Q**. Obviously the Enigma operators would send a whole message at once not one letter at a time.

See fig. [2] my simplified Enigma machine diagram. Bear in mind that every time a key is depressed the complete wiring configuration through the rotors is changed. Therefore if a letter **Q** is typed again a different letter will be illuminated.

With the conclusion of World War I Winston Churchill made a blunder in his reports and a later book (World in Crisis 1911–1918) when he suggested that the breaking of German codes was one of the principal reasons that enabled the British to win the war. Meanwhile in Germany, the department that dealt with German communications for their military headed by Erich Fellgiebel, became aware of Churchill's view. The Germans decided to make sure that if they were ever to be involved in another conflict, their codes and ciphers would remain secure. Therefore the Germans decided to be on the lookout for a new cipher system that was completely and utterly unbreakable.

So who did break the Enigma code? The answer is simple: there is no such thing as an Enigma code. The Enigma had settings each day, which were changed at midnight. Then what is Enigma? There are many technical books explaining all internal workings of the German military M3 Enigma with all its complications and wiring configurations. But we don't need to know that. In the film The Imitation Game, (*Black Bear Pictures 2014)* Alan Turing, played by Benedict Cumberbatch, stated "Enigma was the greatest encryption device in history". It certainly contained extremely clever circuitry that made the Enigma machine reciprocal. That means you can use the same machine for cipher and decipher. In fact each rotor / scrambler was a cipher machine in its own right.

So let's look at the components of the German military Enigma machine M3. The machine weighed 12Kg The main components: Keyboard, Plug board (*stecker* board), Lamp board, Entry disc, Right-hand rotor (No.3), Centre rotor (No.2), Left-hand rotor (No.1), and Reflector disc. The Keyboard was QWERTZU (as opposed to the British QWERTY configuration). Powered by a 4.5 V battery, it was supplied with a monthly or bi monthly setting sheet fig.[1].

The plug board we will also refer to as the *Stecker*. On the front of the M3 are 26 sockets representing letters of the alphabet. Through a set of 10 link cables you can change one letter to another, example: you can link the letter A to the letter V, or you could link the letter C to the letter M, and so forth. This small patch panel is not too dissimilar to an old-fashioned telephone exchange where you are changing lines, in this case you are changing letters. After you have depressed a key on the keyboard the current of electricity will pass through the plug board on its journey to the entry disc.

The current now reaches the entry disc. This is the beginning of the real encipherment as the current will now proceed through the three rotors.

The right-hand rotor receives the current which changes the letter. The rotor will turn one position every time a letter on the keyboard is depressed. It will turn over one notch at a time. After it has turned 26 times that would mean there have been 26 keystrokes then the centre rotor will turn over once. After the centre rotor has turned 26 times the left hand rotor will now turn over once notch. This is similar to the old type analogue gas and electricity meters.

Each rotor has its own individual wiring configuration. There was a box of five different rotors for the German army and air force and there were three extra rotors for the Navy totalling eight. The 26 positions of the rotor are represented by letters of the alphabet. (Some models use numbers 1 to 26)

There is an electrical contact on each side of the rotor which is connected by a different wiring configuration for each rotor. As the current passes through each of the rotors the encryption is enhanced. Each time a rotor advances one notch it attains a different array of electrical contacts.

The current then makes contact with the left hand fixed plate which is known as a reflector (this has a fixed wiring configuration). It will send the current back through the three rotors, on a completely different path. Eventually the current will get back to the original entry disc on the right-hand side of the three rotors. The current will now proceed back to the *stecker* on the front of the M3 Enigma where via the link cable again it will change the letter.

The final path of the current is to the lamp board. The lamp board has the letters in the same order as the keyboard. These are internally illuminated by small lightbulbs: once the current has reached the lamp board the enciphered letter will now appear illuminated. Phew!

From the time you press that initial letter on the keyboard to the lamp lighting up on the lamp board the current has passed through 159 million million million possibilities to produce that enciphered letter.

Ring settings.

We spoke about the rotors turning over one notch every time a keystroke is actioned. It is important to note that the actual turnover point can be adjusted. This means that we can control the particular point at which the rotor turns over. There is a small catch on the side of the rotor which can be manually adjusted as per the daily setting sheets and this will change the turnover point of that particular rotor. This is known as the *Ringstellung* which rotates the barrel of letters around the rotor wheel.

For extra security there were some Enigma machines that had two turnover points on their rotors, but we won't concern ourselves about this today.

It's impossible to break! So the Germans believed.

The main work to break Enigma was carried out by the codebreakers at Hut six and Hut eight at Bletchley Park.

However it must be remembered that most of the early fundamental work of breaking the Enigma was achieved by the brilliant Polish codebreakers during the late 1920s and 1930's The Enigma was always evolving as the Germans were enhancing the security features of the machine. The Polish codebreakers ran out of time and resources. How Bletchley Park took over their story is told in my book. "A journey to station X".

There were many different methods of attempting and succeeding to break into the Enigma system. They included such things as: rodding, the Jeffrey sheets, mathematical algorithms and even the Herival tip. It was not just the Germans who used Enigma. We spoke of early commercial and diplomatic machines, even other sections of the axis war machine used various different types of Enigma. Certainly Italy and Spain had a four rotor Enigma "D" which had no *Stecker* or plug board. Even with four rotors it was quite soon broken by Bletchley Park. Japan later was issued with Enigma type "T" machines. The *Abwehr* were also issued with their dedicated Enigma "G" type machine.

How the codes were broken

We are just going to look at one particular aspect of breaking the Enigma M3 machine which was essentially used by all the German military Navy army and air force. The Germans were told Enigma was impossible to break, but there were too many security instructions which caused a weakness in the system. The setting up procedure is quite a complex affair. Some operators in the German army and air force took shortcuts, and became nonchalant, this form of laziness helped Bletchley Park with the constant supply of cribs or clues. Every cipher system has an apparent weakness and Enigma was no different. Later we will look at some of the errors that the German operators made.

A typical German communications network could consist of a number of separate stations all using the same codebook and settings sheet. If you want to send a message to one station in the group you would have to call them by Morse code with their individual call-sign in plain or un-ciphered text. Once the receiving station has confirmed a communications link, you would now need to synchronise both of your Enigma machines before the main body of the message could be sent.

Three rotors would have been chosen from a box containing five. They would be placed in the Enigma machine in the order indicated by that day's setting sheet. A lid would close down over the rotors and a small window would just expose a letter or number. (Depending on the type of rotor some were alphanumerical some were alphabetical) German operators would now have to synchronise their sending and receiving stations with their individual message key. We will look at the complexity of this later, but part of the procedure required the originating sending station to turn the three rotors into random positions, then typing three random letters from the keyboard. This in turn would produce an encrypted three letter message key indicated on the lamp board of their machine. The idea behind this was that even if the Allies obtained an Enigma machine they would not be able to work out the message key. This would be sent to the receiving station as part of the setup procedure known as the preambles. Their problem was that on many occasions due to complacency or laziness the sending operator would not use random settings as per his instructions. After all the Germans were told Enigma was completely impossible to break so they tended to use their own personal settings. (However this idleness did not happen with the German naval Enigma they were far stricter with their procedures).

Example.

Rotor position	HIT	BER	ENI	FRI
Keystrokes	LER	LIN	GMA	TZX
Crib for Bletchley Park	Hitler	Berlin	Enigma	Fritz

Another weakness in the system is that the operator would start a message every day with the same standard text. "Quiet night nothing to report" or our patriotic Enigma operator may well put at the end of the message. "Heil Hitler" Some operators also used the names of their girlfriends, their own names, German swear words were also used. Another general lapse in security would be if a message relayed from the German high command was sent to two or more networks. An example of this was on

30th January 1943 when Hitler promoted Admiral Karl Doenitz to Grand Admiral. Hitler ordered that the same message of Doenitz's promotion shall be sent across every military network on that day. This was a gift for the codebreakers at Bletchley Park: on that day they broke all Enigma networks.

What the German Cipher bureau failed to appreciate was that more security procedures that you put into the Enigma machine would decrease the possibilities of what the codebreakers had to look for. This made the codebreakers job that much easier. Two simple but real examples of this, one was on the *Stecker* board. The plug settings were never next to each other in the alphabet. For instance, letter A could never be linked with B, or letter M with N. This would greatly reduce the possibilities of the *Stecker* board positions. Another security feature the Germans introduced was that certain rotors would only be used on certain days. This again increased the possibilities of breaking the code.

The biggest failure of the Enigma machine was its inability to produce its own ciphered letter. If you pressed the letter A for example on the keyboard it would produce any other letter in the alphabet but never the letter A. Letter B could never be a B and so forth throughout the alphabet.

The reason for this was simply that the Enigma machine was designed to be reciprocal. If I sent you a message in cipher-text, providing that you had reset your Enigma machine to its original start settings you could input the cipher-text and the original plain text would be revealed. In other words it works in reverse. For the Enigma to have this facility the wiring configurations throughout the machine and throughout all the rotors had to be of certain design as not to create a short circuit. So to design that wiring system no letter could represent itself. So what are the implications of this?

Therefore if you receive a message from an Enigma machine and had a good idea what words may possibly appear in that message, you would also know that your cipher-text and the guessed word could never have the same letters in the same position, see below for an example. In this instance we will use the word ENIGMA" as part of the message "

Cipher-text	S	H	I	I	F	D	T	V	B	
Guess	X	E	N	I	G	M	A	X	X	
Error x				X						

As you can see from the example above the guessed word was ENIGMA. But this cannot be correct as the letter "I" in the cipher-text and the letter "I" in the guess word are the same. The Enigma machine cannot produce its own letter so that is not correct.

But if we slide our guess word across to the right look what happens then:

Cipher-text	S	H	I	I	F	D	T	V	B	
Guess	⇒	X	E	N	I	G	M	A	X	X
Error x										

So now it is possible that the letters "I I F D T V" may represent the word Enigma. This is a very simple explanation, you would of course had to guess that the word Enigma may possibly appear in that message. I will now give you an example of how this would really work.

If you listen to the BBC weather forecast tonight there are certain words that are likely to be in that bulletin. The word weather, would appear. Words such as rain, cloud, sea temperature, air temperature, etc.

We knew from our intelligence services that the Germans had weather ships out in the North Sea and North Atlantic. We also knew that they were broadcasting weather information to the German air force and to the German Navy. For some reason only known to themselves they would put this information into code through their Enigma machines. This meant that each weather station would have to have an Enigma machine and all the relevant codebooks. They tended to send their weather information at regular times. So we would listen out for the words. "Weather forecast", obviously all the words would be in the German language. This is only the first part of breaking the code. I have tried to make it straightforward as possible.

	1	2	3	4	5	6	7	8	9	10	11	12	13	14	15	16
Cipher-text received	H	J	U	D	F	R	T	G	T	S	U	M	K	M	B	C
Guess	W	E	T	T	E	R	V	O	R	H	E	R	S	A	G	E
Error						x										

Now we have the word weather forecast in German, what you see above was a regular crib for the codebreakers at Bletchley Park. The codebreakers were able to develop clues into the system using this method. Basically they would have a guess of what they think might be in the message. But this won't work as the R cannot become R

	1	2	3	4	5	6	7	8	9	10	11	12	13	14	15	16
Cipher-text received	C	H	J	U	D	F	R	T	G	T	S	U	M	K	M	B
Guess	W	E	T	T	E	R	V	O	R	H	E	R	S	A	G	E
Error																

The above example shows that no letter in the cipher text or in the guessed word are the same therefore as this message was from a weather ship transmission this word is possibly the German for 'weather forecast'.

The Enigma keyboard had only letters, so all numbers had to be spelled out. *Eins* or one in German is probably the most used group of German letters anywhere in the language. So the codebreakers had at their disposal what was known as the *Eins* catalogue. This would give them every word in German that contained the word *Eins*. These were also known as cribs and were very useful for the codebreakers. From the crib the codebreakers would set up a menu which was a diagram of how the letters corresponded with each other. This menu along with the message would be taken by messenger to the Bombe room. It was the job of the Wrens to set up Bombe machines. This is only the first part of the code breaking story. So in the next section we will be talking about a machine with an unfortunate name in wartime and certainly nothing to do with high explosives.

1	2	3	4	5	6	7	8	9
B	E	A	C	H	H	E	A	D
E	D	B	G	E	A	H	D	B

Our sample crib is BEACHHEAD

Our sample Menu created from the crib can be used to set up the Bombe

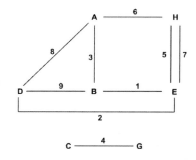

The Bombe Machine

Courtesy The Bombe Re-build Project

At the height of the war there were 211 Bombe machines. There were only six at Bletchley Park, located in Hut 11. The others were distributed between outstations at Stanmore and at Eastcote in Middlesex and there were also a few in some country houses in Northamptonshire and Buckinghamshire. All Bombe machines sites were connected by teleprinter. Behind Hut three at Bletchley Park was the Bombe control room which communicated the information to and from all outstations. In the early part of the war once a menu was created for the Bombe machine it was taken to the Wrens working in Hut 11 who would set up and operate the Bombe machines. The Wrens operated bombe machines at all locations throughout the war.

The Bombe machine was invented by Alan Turing. Though it worked, it wasn't working efficiently. It took far too long to make a stop. A "stop" is the term used when the machine has found the correct settings for that particular network on the day. Fellow codebreaker and mathematician Gordon Welchman devised a clever piece of circuitry known as a diagonal board. Though the board when manufactured was not in fact diagonal the circuit diagram on paper was. This enabled the machine to work extremely efficiently.

The machines were built by the British Tabulating Machine Co. at Letchworth in Hertfordshire. The factory normally built Hollerith tabulating machines. (Post war this company eventually became International Computers limited ICL). The team that built the Bombe machines had no idea what they were building or what the machines were to be used for as all aspects of the machine were built in complete secrecy. The team was led by Harold Doc Keane who liaised with Alan Turing and Gordon Welchman at Bletchley Park.

These machines were not computers they were electro mechanical devices weighing approximately one ton, containing 11 miles of cable, these machines were maintained by RAF engineers. Each Bombe machine represents 36 Enigma machines. Each vertical row of three drums signifies an Enigma. On the centre section to the far right are three black indicator drums which will eventually identify the possible correct result, as in the start position of the Enigma rotors for that particular message. The drums were all different colours to represent the rotor types on the Enigma machine itself. The drums comprised of a similar enhanced wiring configuration of the Enigma rotor.

The Bombe machine would now be set up from the menu obtained from the crib, as we saw in the earlier section. The Wrens would place the drums on the front of the machine. The drums were chosen as a guess of what the actual Enigma rotors could possibly be. As we stated earlier the M3 Enigma had five rotors from which the German operator would choose three as per his setting sheet. This would give the possibility of 60 rotor positions (three out of five rotors to be used in any of the three positions in the Enigma machine $5\times3\times4$). In theory that would mean we would have to use many Bombe machines. The Germans Cipher bureau arranged that the monthly setting sheet would have a restriction of what rotors could be used on which day, which they believed was making the system more secure. What they did not realise was that this greatly reduced the possibilities of which rotors were actually used on any particular day. With some simple mathematical deductions you could guess what the rotor orders were used for that day. If we could reduce the possibilities to 6 drums rather than 60 we would only require two machines to run the job. Once the drums are in position on the front of our Bombe machine, the Wrens now have to set the link cables on the rear of our Bombe. These 26 core cables and connectors are cross plugged as per the menu dictates. The whole setting up of the Bombe machine would take between 15 to 20 minutes. The machine would then be switched on. The drums would rotate in the same fashion as the actual Enigma machine but at a very high speed. The top drum which represents the right-hand rotor on the Enigma machine, turns 26 times faster than the centre rotor. The centre rotor will run 26 times quicker than the bottom rotor that represents the left hand rotor on the Enigma machine.

The machine is switched on and as the drums spin around they are checking every possible Enigma position from AAA to ZZZ the possible permutations being 17,576. As everything is connected electrically, the machine has been designed to stop when it has found the correct settings. Once the machine becomes open circuit our Bombe will finally stop. The Wrens would now have an indication of the actual rotors and *Stecker* settings for our original Enigma intercepted message. The Wrens would now have to test the drums to check whether they are correct, this is done on a checking machine using the original menu. If the check test is satisfactory, our message will be tested on an Enigma machine. As the Bombe operators never had a real Enigma machine to work with, they used a modified version of the British cipher machine called Typex, to emulate the workings of the Enigma. Once again if the findings were correct, the Wren would then type a sample of the message into the Typex machine. They would type in the cipher text, the output results would be printed on a paper tape by the Typex machine. If the printed text was in German the Wrens would know that the settings were correct. The operator calls "jobs up!" The message along with its Enigma settings would be collected by a messenger and taken to Hut 6 for the complete message to be printed out. Message would now be passed to Hut 3 translation analysis and dissemination to the appropriate military authorities.

The above is just an outline into the procedures used for breaking Enigma. The full procedures are much more complex. There are many publications that will describe the full code breaking possibilities of the German military Enigma and the German naval Enigma, which again was even more complex than the army and air force version. Naval Enigma was subject to far more stringent set up procedures. The best way to learn how the Enigma was broken using the Bombe machines is to visit Bletchley Park where they have dedicated volunteer Bombe team operating a rebuilt Bombe machine.

General Heinz Wilhelm Guderian
Communications Truck May 1940
Courtesy Bundesarchiv
Photographer Erich Borchert,
Bild 101I-769-0229-12A

How to set up your Enigma

Sending station.

This next section illustrates the setting up procedure used by German Enigma operator, how he would send his message to a receiving station. We will see that the operator will set his Enigma machine to that day's settings from the monthly setting sheet. fig. 1.

He selects his three rotors from a box of five, as indicated from his setting sheet instructions. Then he adjusts the ring setting on each rotor that indicates the turnover point of each rotor.

He has placed the three chosen rotors in the correct positions inside the machine then closes the lid. Now he will set up his *stecker* to the correct links.

This is known as the ground settings which are now complete.

The operator will now setup his individual key. This is a synchronising process to the station he wishes to transmit to as there are probably several communication posts using that particular setting sheet.

1. He spins his three rotors to a random position and makes a note of the letters in the rotor windows

   WLF

2. Now types on the keyboard three random letters. (Prior to May 1940 he would type them in twice).

   DFG DFG

3. The lamp board illuminates the encrypted letters

   UTE MBV

4. He will now select a new position for his rotors. This will be the Key as in fig. 2   **DFG**

5. Now the operator will send the following information by radio using Morse code to the receiving station, in plain un-enciphered

text. This was known to the British intercept stations as the preambles to a message.

The sending station's *call sign*, which is sending the message

The receiving station *call sign* for whom the message is intended.

Time of origin message

The *number* of characters in the text, *Funfunddreizig* .

Once the receiving operator has confirmed contact and that he has received the preambles, the sending operator would send the **key** that would encrypt the message.

WLF (As in fig.1) **UTE MBV** fig.3

The receiving operator would now change his rotors to **WLF** fig.1

Then the receiving operator will type into the Enigma machine letters **UTE MBV** fig.3

The receiving station's lamp board will illuminate the letters **DFG DFG** fig.2

The receiving operator will now change the rotor positions to **DFG** fig.4

DFG is the key, so now the two stations are synchronised. I realise this is a bit of rigmarole but if you can scan through the procedure a couple of times and you will get the picture.

Both sending and receiving stations now have the same rotor settings **DFG** and they are using the same setting sheet (ground settings). This means both stations are synchronised. Now the main text of the message can be sent.

This procedure is very long-winded, taking three personnel to send and receive a message. One to write the message down, one to operate the Enigma machine and one to operate the radio transmitter. It can be seen that this was a top heavy communications arrangement. Now it is possible to understand the reasons in a war situation, under battle conditions, that message security was compromised. This situation encouraged operators to ignore certain security procedures which gave Bletchley Park an insight into the Enigma system used by the German army and also by the German air force. However the German Navy which includes surface ships and U-boats had a much more stringent procedure for the security of signals. Therefore their messages were much tougher to break into.

German naval Enigma

The German Navy *Kriegsmarine* were far stricter in their procedures for setting up their Enigma machines. There were basically two codebooks used by the German Navy, *Heimisch* for surface ships and U-boats in home waters, *Hydra* for ships in distant waters. The main difference was their choice of rotors. With the army and air force Enigma machines the operators were to choose three rotors from a box of five to comply with their daily setting sheets. However the German Navy had a box of eight rotors, from which they would choose three rotors for their

Enigma machine. Up until February 1942 the basic military Enigma machine M3 was used by all services army, navy and the air force.

This was to change in early 1942, when a four rotor Enigma machine was introduced. Admiral Karl Doenitz, the commander of the U-boat fleet, was concerned that during 1941 the sinkings of Allied merchant ships was on the decrease and the attacks and sinkings of German U-boats was on the increase. Though the German cipher security officers attempted to convince Doenitz that the Enigma system was unbreakable and the bad fortune of the German U-boats was due to aerial reconnaissance and spies in the German U-boat ports. This failed to convince Doenitz and consequently from 1 February 1942 the M4 Enigma was put into use by the U-boats. The Germans called this new code Triton, Bletchley Park named it Shark and therefore was no longer able to read the vital U-boat code.

Bletchley Park was already aware that a four rotor Enigma machine was in use. But it was only being used as a three rotor machine. The forth rotor was kept in a neutral position. The new fourth left-hand rotor was actually a manually turned rotor, basically it was a movable reflector disc. When the keys were pressed on an Enigma machine the fourth rotor never turns over automatically. It was moved manually by the operator as per his instructions on the setting sheet for that particular day. However a few months previous an operator sent a message and accidentally turned the fourth rotor into another position. After the operator sent his message, he had realised his error. The operator then proceeded to send the same message again with the fourth rotor in the correct neutral position, since he was sending his message to another station operating with a three rotor M3 Enigma. By re-sending the same message without resetting the initial set-up procedure, his signal revealed to Bletchley Park that the German U-boats were operating four rotor machines. When the fourth rotor was set into a neutral position it performed as a three rotor machine.

The Germans had now also changed their short signal codebooks and their short weather codebooks. U-boat signals had to be kept short. The Germans knew that long radio messages would be intercepted by British direction finding and give their position away in the matter of seconds. This could lead to the U-boat being attacked by an aircraft or surface ship and being destroyed. German U-boats worked in large packs of possibly 10 to 16 patrolling the North Atlantic. These groups of U-boats were known as wolf packs. As soon as one U-boat spotted a British merchant convoy they would have to signal its position back to their headquarters at Kernevel in the Brittany region of France. To keep this signal short they would use the short weather codebook and the short signal codebook to reduce the length of the radio transmission. Once this message was put into a code it was then put through their Enigma machine. This made the message super-enciphered.

Due to the brilliant work of Alan Turing and his colleagues in Hut 8 at Bletchley Park, the codebreakers were breaking U-boat signals on better than an infrequent basis. After 1st February 1942 this all changed, Bletchley Park could no longer read the U-boat code. Merchant sinkings immediately increased and U-boat attacks were reduced. This caused Bletchley Park major problems. By August 1942 Britain was so badly affected that the country was in dire straits as our supplies of food, fuel and minerals were down to just above bare minimums with just six weeks supplies were left.

Food was in such short supply that rationing was at the smallest allowances. There were very long queues at shops for basic food stuffs. Britain needed a miracle and needed it quick, as it was losing the war and being starved out. The miracle came in the Eastern Mediterranean on 30th October 1942 with the attack on U-boat U-559. A group of extremely brave seamen boarded a sinking enemy submarine and retrieved the vital codebooks that were urgently required. Unfortunately the U-boats sank while 1st Lieutenant Anthony Fasson and Able seaman Colin Grazier were trying to remove a four rotor Enigma from its mountings, they lost their lives in that incident. The recovered code books were immediately sent to Bletchley Park. On 13 December 1942 Bletchley Park was back into the new Triton U-boat code (Shark).

It was realised that four rotor Bombe machines were required. This was going to cost vast amounts of money and resources to build. However the machines were built in the United States by the National Cash register Company. In November 1942 Alan Turing travelled to Ohio in the United States to assist with technical advice. Once the U.S. Bombes were up and running Ultra information was sent to Bletchley Park via the transatlantic cables.

Recovery of all the Enigma the rotors.

It was the Polish codebreakers during the 1930s recovered the wiring configurations of rotors I, II, III. IV, and V, using brilliant mathematical procedures. (full details in book Journey to Station X). Rotors VI and VII were recovered from from U-boat U-33 on 12th February 1940. Rotor VIII from U-13 on 31 May 1940.

If you enjoyed this book you may like to purchase a copy of
A Journey to Station X

Glossary

ASDIC	Anti-Submarine detection Committee
ATS	Auxiliary Territorial Services
C	Chief of MI6
D	Day (the timing for a battle)
	eg: D-2, D-1, D Day, D+1, D+2.
DNI	Director of Naval Intelligence
GC&CS	Government Code & Cipher School
GCHQ	Government. Communications Head Quarters
MI 1b	WW1 Army Codebreaking Section
MI5	Defense of the realm, Home security
MI5 B	Counter-subversion
MI5 B1a	Double Cross section
MI6	see SIS
NID	Naval Intelligence Department
OIC	Operational Intelligence Centre (Admiralty House London)
PWE	Political Warfare Executive
RAF	Royal Air force
SIS	Secret Intelligence Service (MI6).
SHAEF	Supreme headquarters allied expeditionary forces.
SOE	Special Operations Executive
ULTRA	Decrypted messages from Bletchley Park
WAFS	Women's Auxiliary Air Force
WRNS	(Wrens) Women's Royal Naval Service

Bibliography

30 Secret Years	Robin Denniston
Action This Day	Michael Smith
Alan Turing the Enigma	Andrew Hodges
Battle for the Code	Hugh Sebag Montefiore
Bismarck 1941	Angus Konstam
Black Boomerang	Dennis Sefton Delmer
Britain's Best Kept Secret	Ted Enever
British Intelligence in the Second World War	F H Hinsley
Capturing Enigma	Stephen Harper
Code-Breakers	Hinsley & Stripp
Code Book	Simon Singh
Code Name Tricycle	Russell Miller
Colossus 1943 - 1996	Tony Sale
Colossus BP's greatest secret	Michael Smith
Defence of the Realm	Christopher Andrew
Demystifying the Bombe	*Dermot Turing*
Discovery of the Bismarck	Robert Ballard
Double Cross	Ben Macintyre
Finest Years	Max Hastings

Spies Lies and Double-cross Agents

GCHQ	Richard Aldrich
Hitler's Code Breakers	John Jackson
Hitler's Spy Chief	Richard Bassett
HMS Dasher (Secrets of)	J Steele & N Steele
Hut 6 Story	Gordon Welchman
Inside Room 40	Paul Gannon
MI5	Nigel West
MI6 History of MI6	Keith Jeffrey
Second World War	S.P. MacKenzie
Secret History of PWE	David Garnett
Secret Life of BP	Sinclair McKay
Secret War	Michael Smith
Secret Wireless War	Geoffrey Pidgeon
Secrets of HMS Dasher	John & Norman Steele
Seizing the Enigma	David Kahn
Sigint	Peter Matthews
The Secret of Station X	Michael Smith
Ultra goes to War	Ronald Lewin
Wolfpack	David Jordan
World War 2	John Keegan
Zig Zag	Nicholas Booth

Now this is not the end. It is not even the beginning of the end. But it is, perhaps, the end of the beginning.

Winston Churchill

The Lord Mayor's Luncheon, Mansion House

November 10, 1942